Fishy's Flies

Fishy's Flies

Jay "Fishy" Fullum

STACKPOLE
BOOKS

Published by
STACKPOLE BOOKS
5067 Ritter Road
Mechanicsburg, PA 17055
www.stackpolebooks.com

Printed in the United States

10 9 8 7 6 5 4 3 2 1

First Edition

Cover drawings by Jay "Fishy" Fullum
Cover design by Caroline Stover

Library of Congress Cataloging-in-Publication Data
Fullum, Jay.
    Fishy's flies / Jay Fullum.
        p.   cm.
    ISBN 0-8117-2616-9 (alk. Paper)
    1. Flies, Artificial.   2. Fly tying.   I. Title.
SH451.F86 2002
688.7'9124—dc21   2002023065

Contents

Saltwater Creations

Foreword

Magazine editors get a lot of strange things in the mail, particularly if they work for fly-fishing publications. The first package I remember receiving from someone named Fishy Fullum (Fishy?) contained an article about nymphs made with bead-chain eyes, craft-fur bodies, and epoxy-coated Mylar wing cases. They were precisely the sort of trout flies that drive the bamboo-and-Quill-Gordon purists into frenzies of outrage and loathing, so I liked them right away. Besides, the idea and article made sense, the flies were nicely tied, and the photos were patently the work of a guy who knew his way around a camera. Although I had doubts about a grown man going by the name of Fishy, I bought the piece, and it ran in the Autumn/Winter 1996 issue of *Fly Tyer,* of which I was then editor.

More Fishy fly-tying articles followed, each about something just a little strange. I recall a cased-caddis pattern made by coating a hook with epoxy and rolling it in grit from a riverbed. The result looked just like one of the houses that caddis larvae make by gluing together grains of sand and bits of junk with their spit, and it sank, well, like a stone. Gluing sand to a hook is hardly a new idea, but Fishy's use of epoxy made the job much easier, and made for a fly that would bounce off rocks all day without shedding a grain of its dressing. And, again, it pisses off the humorless purists.

Then Fishy sent a bigger package. It contained several exquisite grasshopper flies (made, in characteristic Fishy style, with bits of foam plastic trimmed from a swimming-pool toy) and two pieces of heavy watercolor paper covered with gorgeous step-by-step illustrations and incredibly neat hand-lettered captions. It was, as we say in the trade, a camera-ready piece—an instant article, in other words. The flies were (and still are) the best-looking hoppers I'd ever seen, and the hand-colored, hand-lettered article was the kind of work I didn't think magazines got anymore. An art director might (and ours did) call its look "retro"—not quite old-fashioned, but far from trendy. It was a nifty combination:

an all-synthetic grasshopper fly as modern as this year's umpteen-zillion-modulus graphite fly rods, and a graphic presentation that reminded me of stuff I'd read as a kid. Best of all, the instructions really did teach you how to make the fly and have fun doing it.

The envelope also contained a proposal for an illustrated magazine column called "Creative Tying," which, he promised, would follow the look and spirit of his grasshopper article. I said yes instantly, and Fishy's first "Creative Tying" column ran in the Autumn 1997 issue of *Fly Tyer,* which sported three of his hoppers on its cover. We very quickly ran out of back issues.

Fishy's work has been appearing steadily in *Fly Tyer* and *American Angler* since then, to the delight and edification of readers. He's become a popular figure on the show circuit, and he travels around the country speaking to angling clubs and teaching fly tying. I've made a lot of editorial decisions I look back on with regret, but putting Fishy on as a columnist isn't one of them.

His real name is Jay, and he's a retired graphic artist. You can tell that he's an artist by looking at his flies, of which I'm lucky enough to have a bunch. What you might not discern, unless you look at some of his flies very closely, is how much emphasis he puts on simply having fun with all of this. The word "fun" pops up several times a minute in any conversation with Jay. I have some tiny, balsa-bodied panfish bugs that Fishy made, and I swear that they have expressions on their little faces. They look surprised, like they're squealing "Aaaahhhh!" a split second before a big bluegill eats them. They're fun to look at.

They're also fun to fish with, because, like all of Fishy's creations, they work very well. This is not a guy who ties remarkable flies just for the sake of making people remark on their beauty. I've fished with Fishy a few times, and he can deliver the goods. In a trout stream or a New England bay, on a bass pond or a tropical flat, Fishy catches fish, and almost always with some specimen of his creative tying.

He has as much fun on the water as he does at the vise. He mutters to himself and talks to the fish, coaxing them out of their hidey-holes. "Ooh, it's another one of those *green things*," I remember him saying as he leaned back on a fat, four-pound bass that had eaten some strange, metal-eyed concoction of arctic-fox fur, silicone rubber, and wool. It's a pleasure to watch him handle a fly rod or a canoe; even in the wind, he makes both look easy.

He talks a lot about fishing with his wife, Carol, and, these days, about his grandson, who, of course, is already learning to tie flies. I like a guy who still takes his sweetheart fishing after (I'm guessing here) forty years, and who talks your ear off about his grandson. "Jay is a good man," as a colleague and mutual friend once said.

And he's a hell of a fly tier—curious, inventive, painstaking, skillful. Creative. What you have here are some of the products of that creativity, both at the vise and at the drafting table. You'll learn some new patterns and techniques from Jay's book, but I hope you also learn to see fly tying through his artist's eyes, to see the possibilities in unusual materials and methods.

And I hope that some of Fishy's whimsy and humor rub off on you. These flies are fun, as all fly tying should be. When you run into Fishy at a show, tell him that you had fun with his book. That's all you'll have to say to make him happy.

—Art Scheck
Anderson, South Carolina
January 2002

Introduction

Before retiring to the computer, camera, sketchbook, and fishable waters, I worked for many years designing everything from museum exhibits to the pages of an outdoor magazine. During that time, I learned that a good design can be easily produced from readily available materials. Also, the end product must be functional, and it should offer some benefit to the user. I apply the same guidelines that dictated design projects when I had a "real job" to the flies I present to my quarry.

All the flies in this book were designed to be "tier friendly." All the patterns were created using as few materials as possible. This helps keep the number of steps and the time required to complete each pattern to a minimum. Patterns with more steps or materials do not necessarily catch more fish. They are just more complicated and take longer to tie.

The materials used in these patterns are not exotic, expensive, or difficult to find. Some materials, such as soda straws, sand, plastic canvas, and foam from a youngster's pool toy, may not be found in every fly-tying kit, but even these items are readily available and cost very little. I enjoy designing new patterns that utilize unusual materials. It's fun to make flies with strange stuff, goo, and glue, particularly when that pattern turns out to be a favorite of both the fish and the fly fisher.

After designing and field-testing a new fly, I often lose interest in that particular pattern and move on to new challenges. Since there is room for improvement in every fly pattern, I suggest that you get your creative juices flowing. Tie my flies, improving on the design. Have fun making them better. Nothing makes me happier than to have a fellow tier hand me one of my patterns that has been improved far beyond my original design.

Jay "Fishy" Fullum

Acknowledgments

A special thanks to my wife. Carol has been my best supporter and fishing partner for nearly forty years. Thanks to John Prokorym and Tom Brewster, two great fly tiers, who reviewed the tying segments of the book. I also wish to thank my two daughters, Lisa for her help with the text, and Lori for all of the small stitches.

Terrestrials

Fishy's Foam Hopper

Inch-And-A-Half Worm

Epoxy-Backed Beetle

Epoxy Ant

Fishy's Foam Hopper

As a fly increases in size, more emphasis should be placed on its overall appearance. Many fly tiers lose sight of the importance of size, color, and silhouette when tying larger flies. Consequently, many of these flies don't really look like the larger insects they're meant to imitate, such as grasshoppers.

I had been tying hopper patterns for many years but had taken only a few good trout on them. More often than not, the bigger fish would rise and take a look, but the majority refused the offering. I finally came to the conclusion that my hopper patterns didn't really look like what I had seen jumping ahead of me as I walked along the shoreline of my favorite trout stream.

Taking a fresh look at the real thing was long overdue. So, armed with a small net and a plastic bottle, I went out on a hopper hunt. After my captured specimen had completed its swim in a mixture of water and alcohol, I dried it and took a good look at the size, color, and silhouette of the red-legged grasshopper (*Melanoplis*). Next, I retrieved two terrestrial boxes from my vest and picked out a sampling of the hoppers I'd been fishing. Although these creations looked a little like the specimen, overall, these flies made up of yellow yarn, deer hair, hackle, and knotted sections of turkey quill were rather poor imitations of the real thing.

The size and silhouette of the old hopper patterns weren't too bad, but the color was all wrong. The bodies were too bright and too yellow. The body of the real insect was made up of different shades of gray and dull browns, with only a hint of yellow. Yellow was a good base to start with, but other colors would be required to make the hopper imitation look like the grasshopper lying on my tying bench.

Convinced that a more realistic fly would tempt the larger, more selective fish, I began to redesign the hopper pattern. The body is made from a foam kickboard. These pool toys are about 1 foot wide, 1 1/2 inches thick, and 18 inches long. They're available in bright pink, blue, and yellow; the last is the most useful to fly tiers. You'll find them in the toy or pool supply department of most chain stores during the summer. Use a sharp knife to slice the foam (as you would bread) into pieces 3/16 inch thick. Then cut it into pieces 3/16 inch square. Using scissors, trim the pieces of foam, rounding and tapering one end. Cut it off about 1 1/4 inches from the trimmed end.

Once I was satisfied with the new hopper, I field-tested it on several of Montana's best trout streams.

Montana had been very dry that summer, and the hopper population had exploded. The fish were used to seeing these large insects, as well as a lot of hopper imitations, on the water. Consequently, they weren't easily fooled. Imitations had to be realistic and well presented, or they were refused. This particular hopper pattern was without question the most productive one my partner and I fished during the trip.

Since returning to New York and my local streams, I have seriously fished this hopper. Eastern trout also take the pattern, often gulping it off the surface as if they had not eaten in weeks. On occasion, I still fish the traditional patterns, but when the larger trout become a little more selective, I tie on one of my realistic foam hoppers. This drab-colored pattern is a bit more difficult to see on the water, but the trout don't seem to have any problem finding it. They take this more realistic pattern when other hoppers are just looked at.

Materials List

HOOK:	#6 or #8, 2XL.
THREAD:	Yellow 3/0 flat waxed.
BODY:	Foam from a pool kickboard (see text).
LEGS:	Speckled olive Sili-legs (Wapsi).
WING:	Any porous, synthetic, trim-to-shape wing material. (See the wing for the Adult Stonefly.)
WATERPROOF MARKERS:	Gray, brown, and black to color the body.
FINGERNAIL POLISH:	Light green on the belly, brown on top of the head. Black also used for eyes.
FIVE-MINUTE EPOXY:	Used to secure the foam to the hook, and on the sides and top of the head.
NEEDLE:	With an eye large enough to accommodate the Sili-legs.

1. Wrap the hook shank with yellow 3/0 tying thread. Position the foam body on top of the hook, and make a couple of soft wraps around the foam at the rear of the hook. It's very important to make soft wraps when tying on the foam. If you put too much pressure on the thread when wrapping it around the body, the thread will cut into the material, weakening or ruining the body.

2. Lift the foam piece slightly, and wrap the thread forward to the halfway position on the hook shank, then make several more soft wraps around the foam.

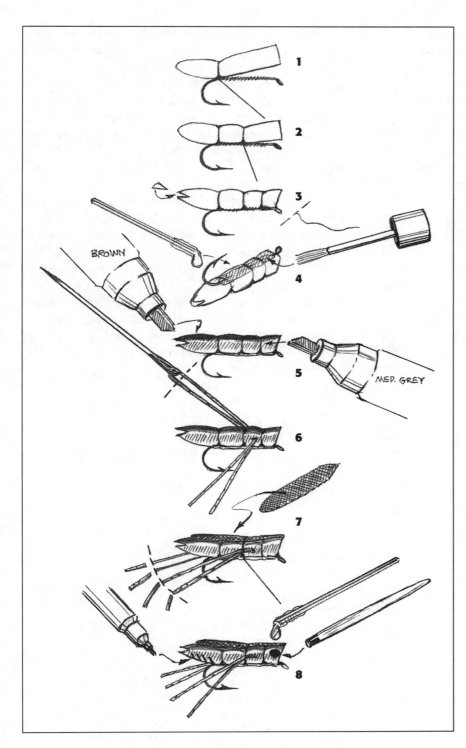

4. Apply a small amount of five-minute epoxy along the hook shank and the bottom of the hopper, but not on the foam extending beyond the bend of the hook. After the epoxy has hardened, color the area with light green fingernail polish.

5. Color the foam body with markers. Medium gray is used on the sides of the fly. Brown is used to color the top of the hopper.

6. Thread the full length of one Sili-leg through the eye of a needle. Divide the material in half, then push the needle through the foam. Cut the Sili-leg behind the eye of the needle to remove it.

7. Reattach the thread at the middle of the hook, then pull the legs back along the sides of the body and make several soft wraps around the area to secure them in place. After the legs are in place, trim them to length. Note that the legs extend slightly beyond the rear of the body.

If you wish, you can tie off the thread at this point, apply a little head cement to the thread, and fish the pattern without the wing. The fish don't see the wing from their vantage point, and I have had good results fishing wingless hoppers. I like to tie some with a wing, however, since they look a little more realistic lying in my fly box. If you prefer to add the wing, complete the next step. Position the wing material on top of the body; secure with several soft wraps of thread; then advance the thread forward to the next segment, make a couple more wraps, and tie off.

8. Coat the top and sides of the head and around the thread at the base of the legs with five-minute epoxy. After the epoxy has hardened, paint the top of the head with brown fingernail polish, then paint on the eyes. Segment the bottom of the abdomen with a fine black marking pen to complete the hopper.

3. Advance the thread, and make more soft wraps to form the third segment of the body, halfway to the eye of the hook. Advance the thread, stopping just behind the eye of the hook. Compress the foam, and catch a little of the bottom of the material. Make a couple of tight wraps, and tie off. Cut a notch in the end of the foam to complete this step.

Inch-and-a-Half Worm

One summer while wading along a stretch of my favorite trout water, I noticed a bright green caterpillar floating on the water ahead of me. I moved slightly to my right and retrieved it. After examining the caterpillar for several minutes, I tossed it back upstream into the head of a small pool. The caterpillar hit the water with a splash, then floated back to the surface. To my surprise, it hadn't drifted more than a few feet when a nice brown trout sipped the large terrestrial off the surface and disappeared back into the dark water on the far side of the pool.

I looked, but I knew I had nothing that would match the large terrestrial. The inchworms in one of my fly boxes were the right color, but the caterpillar the trout had taken was huge compared with them. I tried one anyway, then several more patterns, drifting them over the spot where the trout had taken the caterpillar. After the fourth pattern was refused, I made a mental note to add a large caterpillar imitation to my inventory of terrestrials.

Since my first encounter with that large caterpillar, the original design has changed several times. As new materials became available, I redesigned the fly. A recent change came shortly after I purchased a couple of packs of mini-rubber legs. I had never been happy with the Palmer-style hackle used to simulate the hairy portion of this immature insect. After several failed attempts, I came up with the technique used to tie in the legs. It takes a little longer, but these legs make the caterpillar look much more like the real thing.

Ants, beetles, jassids, crickets, hoppers, and inchworms are often presented to fish, but most of these flies are rather small. Fly fishers, particularly those fishing for stream trout, are reluctant to tie a terrestrial pattern larger than a #12 onto the end of a tippet. In recent years, I have found that a wide variety of fish will take large terrestrials. Each season I catch many trout, smallmouth bass, and panfish on large ants, my foam hoppers tied on #6s and #8s, beetle patterns tied on #8s and #10s, and this caterpillar imitation tied on a #6 streamer hook.

Materials List

HOOK:	#6 streamer hook.
THREAD:	Yellow 3/0 flat waxed.
BODY:	Any closed-cell foam. I prefer the same yellow foam used for Fishy's Foam Hopper.
LEGS:	Black mini-rubber legs (Spirit River).
PAINT:	Tan or light green on belly. Fingernail polish works well.
WATERPROOF MARKERS:	Greens and browns on top and sides.
SUPERGLUE:	Used to secure body and legs.

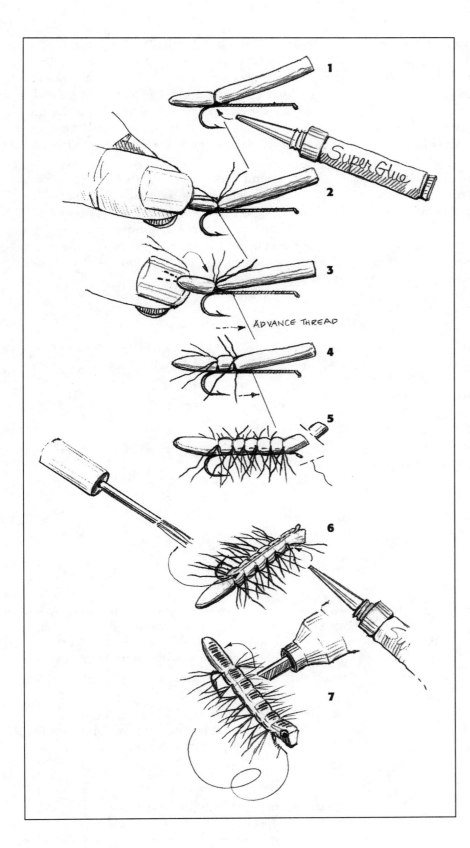

1. Begin by cutting a piece of close-celled foam about 1/4 inch thick and wide and 2 inches long. After trimming the corners off the piece and rounding one end, tie it onto the rear of the hook with two or three soft wraps of thread. Check to see that the foam is positioned directly on top of the hook. Then apply a tiny drop of superglue to the base of the thread, and allow the glue to dry. Gluing the body to the top of the hook prevents the foam body from turning on the hook shank, making the following steps easier.

2. Cut the mini-rubber leg material into 3/4-inch lengths. Position two of these pieces along the front side of the foam, and make two wraps to capture the legs.

3. Unwrap the thread a quarter turn, position two pieces of the leg material along the back side of the foam, then make two additional wraps of thread to secure these legs. After the legs have been secured, lift the foam slightly and advance the thread to the next segment of the caterpillar.

4. Tie in another set of legs, and advance the thread.

5. Continue this process, working forward until the entire body is completed. Then cut off the excess foam and tie off the thread.

6. Apply a little superglue along the hook shank and at the points where the legs extend from the sides of the body. After the glue has dried, paint the underside of the caterpillar.

7. Color the sides and top of the fly with markers. The caterpillar can be colored in many shades of either brown or green. The silly-looking painted eyes are optional.

Epoxy-Backed Beetle

Many of my new terrestrial patterns have been designed after beating the bushes. I would spread a sheet on the ground under some foliage, then beat on the branches with a stick, causing many of the resident insects to fall onto the sheet. I would then sort through the critters in an effort to determine what was falling into the stream each time the wind blew through the canopy.

Most of the insects I found crawling on the sheet were ants, but I also found hundreds of other insects, including many species belonging to the order Coleoptera. This was no surprise, since a third of all known insects residing on this planet belong to this order. With more than 30,000 species of beetles in North America, I determined that the trout had to be taking hundreds of beetles off the water each season. Less than a week later, I added several new beetle patterns to my terrestrial box.

Since adding these larger, more lifelike beetles to my inventory, I have taken many good fish. However, soon after I decided to write an article about them, I determined that the original design was a bit too complicated. I sat down at the vise and went to work simplifying the pattern. After a few failed attempts, I was able to eliminate one of the major steps without changing the end result. In fact, the new pattern looked better than the original.

Utilizing this tying method, I made up a few examples using a National Audubon Society field guide as a reference. It was fun tying imitations of a nine-spotted ladybug, a common black ground beetle, and a Pennsylvania firefly. They are all very fishable, productive patterns. I even tied an elephant stag beetle just for the fun of it. I doubt it will ever end up on the end of a line.

I recommend that you tie a few of these larger, more lifelike beetles. Vary the shape and size of the foam, the amount of epoxy applied over the top of the body, and the color. Remember that there are tens of thousands of different beetles out there. No matter what you come up with, it will probably look like one of them.

Materials List

HOOK:	#14 to #6. Vary the size and length of the hook shank to accommodate the body of the particular beetle you're tying.
THREAD:	Tan, brown, or black 6/0 waxed (match the color of the foam).
BODY:	Sheet foam (available at craft stores or fly shops in a wide range of colors, with black, tan, and brown being most useful).
LEGS:	Flexi-floss or any similar material.
PAINT:	Fingernail polish works well.
FIVE-MINUTE EPOXY, SUPERGLUE, AND ZIP KICKER:	Used for the body.

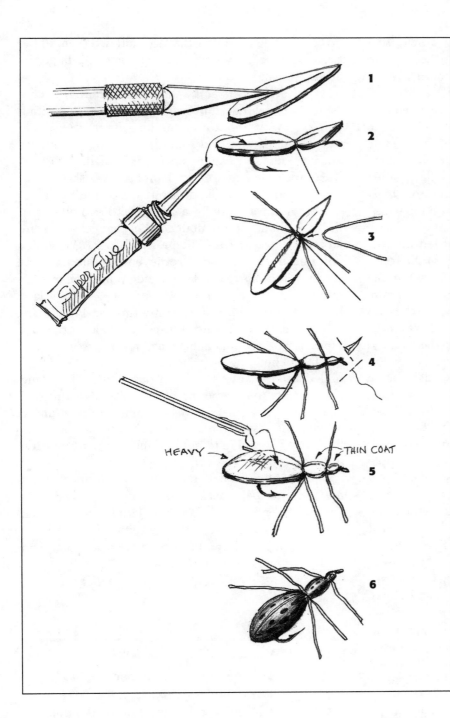

1. Cut the sheet foam to shape with scissors. Then make a cut down through the center of the body material to accommodate the hook shank, but don't split the foam from end to end.

2. Cover the hook shank with thread, stopping at the center of the hook. Attach the foam body to the top of the hook. Apply a drop of superglue to the opening in the rear portion of the foam body, then gently pull on the rear of the body to seat the hook shank in the middle of the foam, and apply a drop of Zip Kicker (an accelerator that dries the superglue).

3. Tie in two legs on either side of the body.

4. Advance the thread, and make several wraps around the foam. Tie in the remaining legs. Advance the thread, and make several wraps around the foam just behind the eye of the hook. Remove the excess foam, and tie off the head.

5. Apply a thin coat of five-minute epoxy to the head and thorax of the beetle, then a *heavy* coat of epoxy to the top of the beetle's abdomen. A little epoxy is also applied under the foam body to secure it to the hook. Turn the beetle in the vise or on a drying wheel until the epoxy hardens.

6. After the epoxy has hardened, paint the beetle to your specifications.

Epoxy Ant

Ineeded a few slides to accompany an article, so I called my friend John Prokorym and asked him to join me on the water. This particular time, I needed fisherman shots, not fish pictures, so I wouldn't be bringing along a rod. John would have the stream to himself. Even though I had to work, I didn't want to ruin John's chances of catching a few of the feeding trout, so I decided to set up where there was some cover between the camera and the fish. A large fallen tree stump along the bank would hide me from view but get me within camera range of John and the water, without putting the trout off their feed.

I kept as low as possible as I approached the tree stump. Once there, I peeked over the top of the roots. The trout were feeding several yards away. I set up the camera and waited as John worked his way upstream. A moment later, I felt something slowly crawling up my arm. It was an ant—a very large ant. For the next few minutes, my thoughts turned to the activity on the tree trunk. It was like a parade. There were ants everywhere. Some were smaller #14s and #16s, but a couple of them were huge.

John took several good fish on the smaller ant patterns during the photo expedition. In fact, the fishing had been so good that we decided to return the next afternoon. That following morning, I checked my supply of ants. The lower left-hand corner of my terrestrial box contained only a couple of my favorites. I needed to tie up a dozen or so before we returned to the stream.

After tying a supply of the #14s and #16s, I decided to make up several ants to match the larger ones I'd seen parading across the tree trunk. I started out using foam for the body, but after the black paint was applied, the body looked rough, not smooth and glossy like the ants I'd seen the day before. Even though it would take longer, since it involved more steps and some drying time, I decided to try a technique I'd used when tying other large terrestrial patterns. I trimmed several pieces of foam to shape, then tied the pieces onto the rear portion of the hooks. I coated the foam pieces with five-minute epoxy and put them on the drying wheel to harden. After the epoxy was hard, I painted the bodies and returned them to the wheel. Once the paint was dry, I tied a smaller piece of foam onto the front portion of the hooks and repeated the epoxy and paint technique. The quality of these large ant bodies was much better. The finish was smooth and glossy like the real thing. I split a strand of black Flexi-floss, cut three pieces for the legs, and tied them in between the two body sections to complete this large, realistic ant pattern.

When we arrived at the stream that afternoon, conditions were wonderful. A strong wind was depositing edible morsels onto the water, and the trout were actively feeding. John and I started out using the smaller ant patterns and caught an occasional fish, but we were not doing as well as I thought we should be, considering how well the trout were feeding. I decided that it was time for a change and tied on one of the larger ants. John noticed the change when the larger ant hit the water like a small rock. "What did you put on?" he asked. I retrieved the line and cast the fly within his reach. He picked up the leader, took one look at the ant, and informed me, "It's too darn big." I just smiled, retrieved my line, and made another cast. The leader turned over and the ant "splashed down," making a ring on the glassy surface. As I watched the ring increase in size, the water boiled and the ant was gone. I raised the rod tip, and a good-size trout came out of the water like a rocket. For a few moments, the fish would not allow me to shorten the distance between us, but finally the trout tired and I was able to net it, unhook it, and return it to the water.

"Catch him on that monster ant?" John asked. I nodded and went back to my fishing. Several casts later, another trout inhaled the offering, then another. After I'd caught and released the sixth fish, John could resist no longer. "Got another one of those things, and what's it going to cost me?" he asked.

continued on p. 10

Materials List

HOOK:	Mustad 94831, #10 or #12.
THREAD:	Any color for the body portion; black 6/0 for tying on the legs.
BODY:	Any closed-cell foam. I prefer the stuff used to make kickboards and other pool toys.
LEGS:	Black Flexi-floss. Split the material in half. (Fine, black rubber legs can also be used.)
PAINT:	Black fingernail polish works best.
FIVE-MINUTE EPOXY:	Used to coat the foam body.

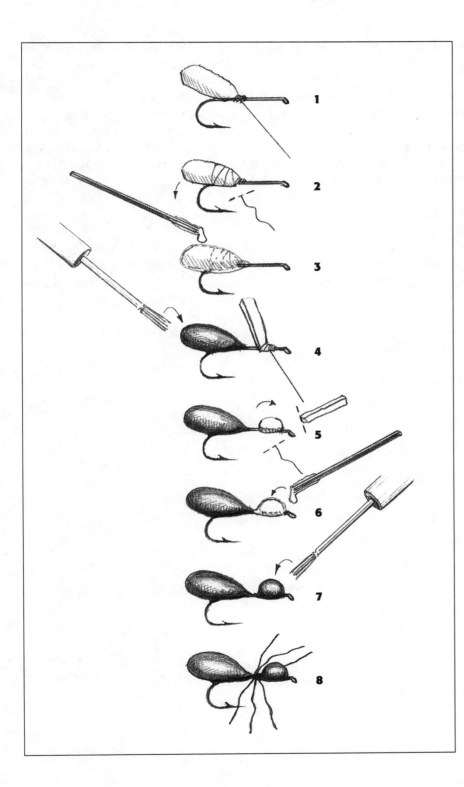

1. Cut the piece of foam to shape, attach the thread, and tie the front portion of the foam piece onto the hook shank.

2. Make a couple of soft wraps around the body to secure the body against the hook, return to the front of the foam, and tie off the thread.

3. Coat the foam with five-minute epoxy, and put the fly on the drying wheel until it hardens.

4. After the epoxy has hardened, paint the body and return it to the wheel. Let the body dry thoroughly before you continue. Once it is dry, start the remainder of the body by tying in a short length of foam.

5. Pull the foam forward and secure it with several wraps of thread, remove the excess foam, and tie off.

6. Coat the front portion of the body with epoxy, being very careful not to fill in the gap between the two sections of the body.

7. Paint the front portion of the body. Again, be careful not to fill in the gap between the two sections.

8. Split the black Flexi-floss in half, and tie in three pieces to form the legs. Tie off the thread and add a drop of head cement to complete the pattern.

"Lots of steps—foam, epoxy, and paint—got to be worth at least five bucks," was my response. Once again I cast the ant within his reach. He cut it off the end of my tippet and changed flies. Before I could retrieve my line, locate another ant, and tie it onto the end of my line, John had a fish on.

When I began fishing these large ants, I was concerned about presentation. Often the low, gin-clear water conditions make it necessary to fish leaders tapered down to a 6X tippet. I was pleasantly surprised to find that the large ant doesn't turn over as badly as I expected. The fly still hits the water like a rock, but after fishing these large ants for several seasons, I now believe that this "splashdown" actually attracts the trout's attention rather than spooking them, since many strikes come seconds after the ant hits the water.

These ants are more productive than most other ant patterns, since the additional weight of the epoxy and paint makes it look more like the real thing when it's presented to the fish. The foam keeps these ants afloat, but the combined weight of the hook, epoxy, and paint causes the fly to float *in* the water, not *on* the water. If you capture the real thing and drop it into a container of water, you'll see that the ant doesn't stay on top. Like most land-dwelling insects, ants don't walk on water, they swim in it, like we do.

Note: This tying technique can also be used for slightly smaller ants. Just be careful when applying the epoxy. If you use too much, the smaller ants will sink rather than floating in the surface film.

Dry Flies

Foam-Backed Humpy

Adult Stonefly

Cranefly

Foam-Backed Humpy

The Humpy or Goofus Bug isn't usually fished to a specific hatch. It's tied onto a tippet when the angler wants to present a fly that will float when other dry flies won't. The Humpy's deer- or elk-hair tail, dubbed fur, shellback made from more hair, hairwing, and heavy hackle all work to keep this pattern on top of the water. However, even after the traditional Humpy is treated with floatant, in time it will soak up water and refuse to stay on the surface.

While experimenting with materials that might make this fly float longer, I decided to try a little high-density foam. At first, I tied the foam directly onto or around the shank of the hook. Doing so produced a fly that would float, but the unique silhouette of the Humpy was lost. After several more failed attempts, I tied a strip of foam over the top of the dubbed fur body. This worked very well. In fact, the foam did such a good job of keeping the Foam-Backed Humpy afloat that there was no need for the hairwing or the stiff, dry-fly-quality hackle.

The Foam-Backed Humpy is much easier to tie than the traditional pattern. I sometimes had a little difficulty tying the old-style Humpy, particularly when estimating the length of the clump of hair that ended up being divided to form the wings. Every once in a while, the wings on my flies were lost somewhere in the hackle or extended too far above the tips of the hackle. The only proportions the tier really needs to be concerned with when tying the Foam-Backed Humpy are the length of the tail and the size of the hackle feather.

Before I present the Foam-Backed Humpy to fish, I work a little floatant into the hair, fur, and hackle, and especially the foam. I use a gel-type floatant, working it into the foam by gently squeezing the fly between my fingers. One application of floatant keeps the fly on top all day.

Materials List

HOOK:	#10 to #14 standard dry fly.
THREAD:	Tan or brown 6/0.
BODY:	Foam over a dubbed body. I prefer tan, olive, or bright orange poly dubbing.
TAIL:	Natural deer tail (stacked).
HACKLE:	Any halfway decent reddish brown hackle. (Save your better-quality dry-fly hackle for more conventional dry flies.)

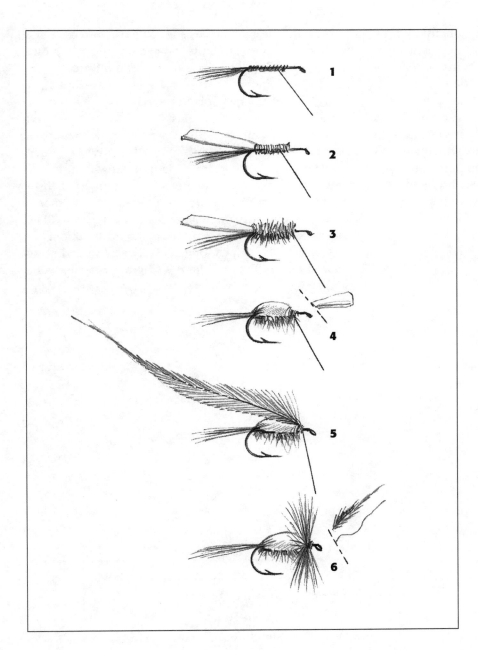

1. Attach the thread, and tie in the tail.

2. Using a sharp knife, cut lengths of foam approximately 1/4 inch wide and 1/8 inch thick. Trim the end of the strip to a point, then tie it onto the top of the hook. Bind it down all the way back to the base of the tail.

3. After tying on the foam, twist dubbing onto the thread and form the body. Leave room at the front to tie off the foam and wind on a bushy hackle.

4. Pull the foam forward, stretching it over the top of the dubbing, and secure it behind the eye of the hook with several wraps of thread. Trim off the excess.

5. Bind down the stub of foam, and attach the hackle.

6. Wrap four or five turns of hackle. Tie off the feather, and remove the excess. Wind a neat head, and tie off the thread. Apply a drop of head cement to complete the fly.

Adult Stonefly

Many tiers seem to favor tying the stonefly nymph, and the reason is obvious: They are handsome critters, and they catch fish. But I was interested in a simple pattern that would imitate the adult.

Unlike members of many other orders of aquatic insects, the stonefly adult looks like the nymph with wings. Two sets of rather large wings are encased on the back of the nymph. After the nymph wiggles out of its shuck, these large wings become functional, giving the insect the ability to fly like a tiny helicopter moments before crashing. Adult stoneflies are not the best fliers.

With this design, the large wings have always been a problem. Earlier attempts twisted the tippet, didn't hold up for very long, or were too complicated to tie. Finally, a homemade wing material I developed for Fishy's Foam Hopper solved the wing problem on the adult stonefly (see Materials List). To make it, you stretch interfacing over the open top of a cardboard box and secure it with pushpins. Brush two or three coats of Aero-Gloss onto the fabric, allowing it to dry between coats. After the Aero-Gloss has dried thoroughly, the material can be cut into hundreds of pieces using a metal straightedge and an X-acto knife. The pieces for this particular pattern should be about $1/4$ inch wide and $7/8$ inch long. This fly can be tied using your choice of brown, black, and gray materials. The same wing material is used on all the patterns.

Materials List

HOOK:	#6 or #8 standard nymph hook.
THREAD:	Brown or black 6/0.
TAIL:	Brown goose biots.
RIB:	Small, round, tan vinyl ribbing.
ABDOMEN:	Fine brown dubbing.
LEGS:	Black mini-round rubber.
WING:	Cardboard box, two dozen pushpins, small disposable foam brush, 3.5-ounce bottle of clear Aero-Gloss Airplane Dope (used to build model airplanes; available at hobby stores), 1 yard plain black interfacing (available at fabric stores).
THORAX:	Black E-Z Shape Sparkle Body to coat top and bottom.

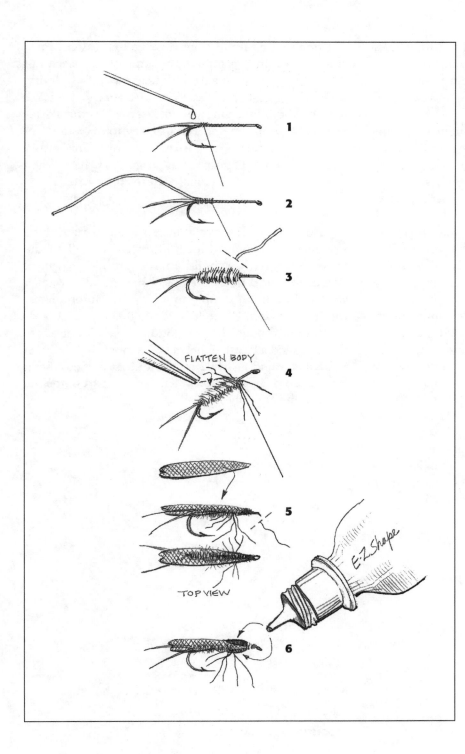

FLATTEN BODY

TOP VIEW

E-Z Shape

1. Begin the pattern by attaching the thread, then tie in a pair of goose biots to form the split tail. Apply a drop of head cement to the base of the tail to prevent the biots from changing position.

2. Tie in a short length of small, round, tan vinyl ribbing.

3. Cover about two-thirds of the hook shank with the fine brown dubbing, tapering the body slightly, then complete the rib and tie it off.

4. Flatten the body with a pair of smooth-jawed pliers, then tie in three lengths of black mini-round rubber to form the legs.

5. Trim the wing material to the desired shape with scissors. Tie in the wing, finish the head, and tie it off. The top view shows how the wing extends beyond the back of the hook. The wing should also extend back over half the length of the tail.

6. Apply a little black E-Z Shape Sparkle Body under the thorax at the base of the legs and on top of the thorax to complete the adult stonefly.

Cranefly

Through the years, I've turned over hundreds of rocks in an attempt to identify the aquatic insect life on the bottom of a stream. This is a rather common practice. Fly fishers who enjoy the pursuit of stream trout often inventory the stream bottom to find out what might be on the trout's menu during a particular outing, but few anglers survey the insects inhabiting the foliage along these same waters. I, however, have spent hours "beating the bushes" along trout streams, and, as expected, the majority of the terrestrials I found were ants, followed by beetles, spiders, caterpillars, and dozens of other interesting insects, including flies from the family Tipulidae. I wondered if the trout were also finding these craneflies on the water. Nothing in my fishing vest was tied specifically to represent these long, spindly legged flies. Would it be worth the time and effort to design a cranefly pattern? And if I did come up with a fishable cranefly, would the trout take it?

I accepted the challenge, but as expected, my first few attempts failed. They resembled the natural, but the flies did not hold up very well when taken by trout. Casting was enough to destroy some of the early designs. Finally, I decided to dispense with the natural materials I had been using for the wing and legs and try some of the more durable synthetics. A bit of Z-Lon, a few lengths of knotted Flexi-floss, and a little superglue were combined to make this durable, productive cranefly pattern.

I don't know if the trout mistake this pattern for a cranefly, a spider, a spinner, or some other insect, but they take it. I soak this fly with floatant and fish it dry. Like most fly fishers, I like to see the quarry as it takes my offering off the surface, but even when this fly refuses to stay on top and I'm too lazy to dry it and recoat it with floatant, it still catches trout. This rather unconventional pattern often triggers strikes when some of the more traditional patterns have failed.

Adult craneflies are not really terrestrials. Like stoneflies or mayflies, their life cycle is tied to the water. Years back, I found a large, grublike worm in one of the local trout streams. I had no idea what it was, so I took the sample to an aquatic entomologist for identification. When he told me that it was a cranefly larva, I thought he was kidding. The larva, commonly called a "leather jacket," was more than $1/4$ inch in diameter and nearly 2 inches long. It is still difficult for me to imagine that this huge larva is part of the life cycle of the cranefly.

Materials List

HOOK:	#10 or #12 standard dry-fly hook.
THREAD:	Gray 6/0 or 8/0.
ABDOMEN:	Cream poly dubbing.
LEGS:	Orange Flexi-floss, Super Floss, or Spanflex.
THORAX:	Dun poly dubbing.
WINGS:	White Z-Lon. Superglue to position the wings.

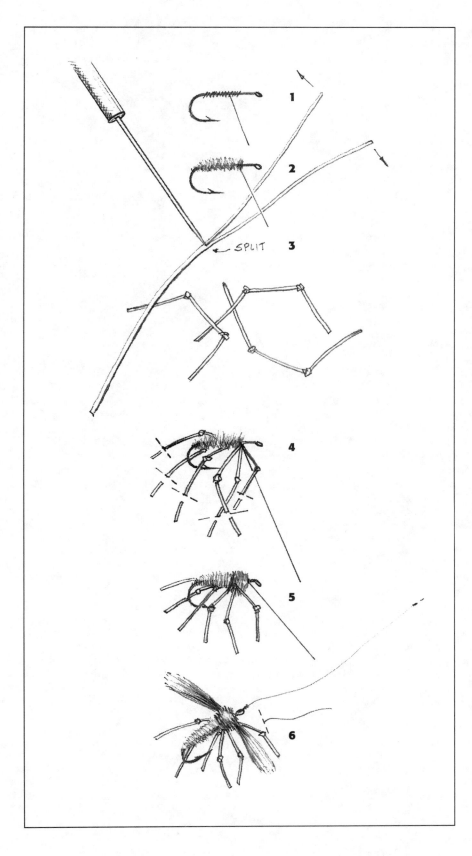

1. Attach the thread.

2. Cover the first two-thirds of the hook shank with cream dubbing.

3. Stick the point of a bodkin into the orange Flexi-floss, and divide the strand in two. Next, cut the strand into three pieces and tie the knots. The knots should be tied near the center of the strand, about $3/8$ inch apart.

4. Tie in the legs, then trim them to length. Be careful not to trim them too short. Remember, the dominant feature of this fly is its long, spindly legs. It's easier to tie on all the legs at the same time. Don't worry about making them perfect. The legs of the cranefly are delicate, and they tangle when the fly ends up on the water.

5. Tie in the thorax using a fine dun-colored dubbing. Start the dubbing in front of the legs while holding them back, then pull the legs forward and wrap a little of the dubbing behind the legs. Once the thorax has taken shape, make a final wrap forward, returning the thread just behind the eye of the hook.

6. Tie in a length of Z-Lon just behind the eye of the hook, then tie off the thread. Apply a little superglue to the base of the wings, then pull on the tips of the wings as the glue dries. This keeps the wings narrow. After the glue is completely dry, trim the wings to shape as shown in the drawing. When cutting a length of Z-Lon for the wing, cut the piece about $1 3/4$ inches long. This is far more than you need, but the longer length enables you to hold the tips of the Z-Lon without gluing your fingers to the wing.

Bass Flies

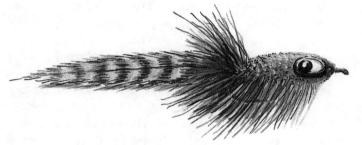

Hair-Guard Bass Fly

T. P. Stickleback

Woolhead

Red Dragonfly

Baby Crayfish

Hair-Guard Bass Fly

I had already completed several deer-hair flies and was about to make the first cut with the razor blade on the last one, when I had an idea. Rather than trimming the hair flat and close to the bottom of the hook, I wondered what would happen if I trimmed it flat on the sides. I trimmed the hair off the sides as close to the hook as I dared and then tapered the hair along the top of the fly. The haircut looked a little strange, but if the hair left along the bottom of the hook was enough to make the creation "weedless," it might be worth field-testing. I tied three more of these strange-looking creations and added them to my box of hair-bodied bass bugs.

Several days later, while casting some of my old favorites at the shoreline, I happened to remember the hair-guard flies. I tied one onto the leader and cast it toward the cover. It didn't cast any better or any worse than the other large hair bugs, but the action in the water was terrible. The fly lay on its side and didn't look very exciting when retrieved. After a couple more casts, I returned the fly to the box.

Several weeks later, a friend invited me to fish a bass pond he had gained access to earlier in the season. He advised me to pack light, since we would be fishing out of his very small canoe. I packed my favorite 8-weight outfit and a small fly box and was at his house bright and early the next morning. An hour later we were on the water.

The pond had the reputation of holding a good number of sizable largemouths, but getting to them was going to be a problem. The entire pond was a maze of downed trees and weed cover. There was no way that we were going to be able to fish a fly unless it was weedless. I hadn't brought my large bag, which of course contained the box with all the bass bugs tied with monofilament and wire weedguards. I asked my fishing partner if he had brought along any weedless bass bugs, but he didn't have a single one with him, either. As I picked through my small box searching for something—anything—I could use, I came across the hair-guard flies. I didn't have any confidence in the fly, but it was the only one I could fish without picking up a pound of weeds with every cast. Reluctantly, I tied one on and tossed another to my partner. He gave me a strange look, shook his head, and tied the fly onto the end of his leader.

I was about to apologize, when my friend groaned and pulled back hard on the rod. A moment later, a very nice bass boiled in the surface. The largemouth made a valiant attempt to throw the strange fly embedded in its lower jaw, but the hook held, and the first bass of the day was caught and released.

I still wasn't convinced that this fly was worth fishing, even though one bass had taken it. I tried hard to concentrate on what I was doing. I cast into several good-looking pockets of cover and tried to make the fly look like it was "edible." On the next cast, I had retrieved the fly only a few feet when something moved under the weeds behind it. I let it lie still on top of the weeds, then gave a little tug on the line, just enough to wiggle the fly. The instant the fly moved, the water exploded. I struck, and the link between angler and fish straightened. Putting all the pressure I dared on the tippet, I coaxed the bass out of the dense cover. Finally, after a lengthy battle, the fish was brought close to the side of the canoe. A few weeds on the leader had added to the weight, but what had been doubling the rod was a respectable largemouth. I was beginning to change my mind about this strange-looking bass fly.

I still don't like the action of the hair-guard fly when it's retrieved, but it is weedless, and the bass seem to think it's great. Far too often, the angler decides whether a particular fly looks the way it should in or on the water. Realistically, we should let the fish determine whether a fly is worth fishing. The bass have decided that they like the hair-guard fly. Consequently, so do I.

Materials List

HOOK:	#1/0 to #4/0 4XL.
THREAD:	White 3/0 flat waxed nylon.
BODY:	Natural deer body hair, spun, packed, and trimmed.
TAIL:	Four grizzly hackles.
COLLAR:	Two grizzly hackles.
EYES:	Doll eyes attached with five-minute epoxy.

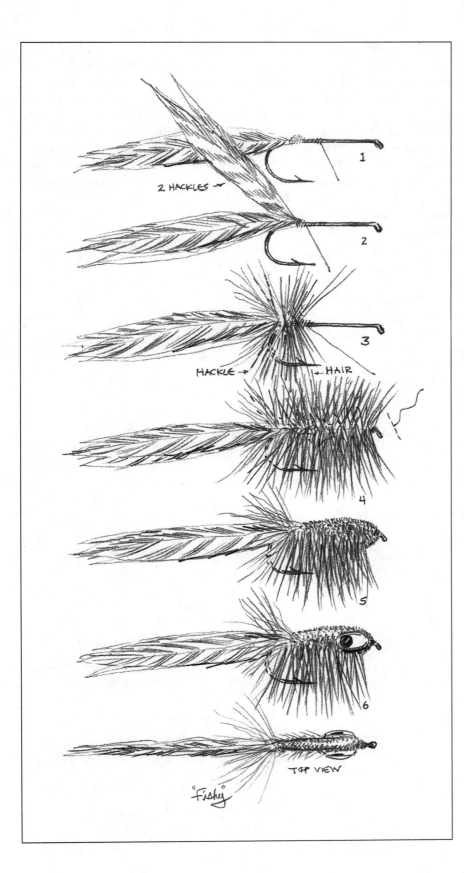

1. Attach the thread, then tie in four grizzly hackles for the tail.

2. Tie in two more of the same hackle to the base of the tail.

3. Wrap the hackles to form a collar, tie off, and remove the excess. Then start building the spun deer-hair body.

4. Continue spinning hair until the entire hook shank is covered, then tie off the thread and add a drop of head cement.

5. Using a razor blade, trim off the hair along both sides of the hook shank, then trim the top of the fly, tapering the hair back until you reach the collar. Do not trim along the hook gap or the bottom of the hook.

6. Attach the eyes using a little five-minute epoxy to complete the streamer.

Woolhead

I tied the fly onto the end of the tippet, cast it down along the side of the canoe, then retrieved it a few feet to see what this new creation looked like in the water. I was not impressed. My great-looking woolhead streamer resembled a dead stick.

Since I'd spent over an hour tying up several of these flies, I decided to fish the "dead stick" for a while to see if any of the bass or northern pike in the area were interested. After the fly had been in the water for a few minutes, I lifted it out to make the next cast. Again, I made a short cast and retrieved the streamer back toward the canoe. I was shocked. Each time I put a little pressure on the line, the streamer crawled through the water as if it were alive.

Since my first experience with streamers tied primarily of wool and arctic fox tail, I have learned to soak them before presenting them to the fish. The addition of Sili-legs in the tail of this particular pattern puts some action into the fly the second it hits the water. However, it is still a good idea to hold it in the water and squeeze it in your fingers before making that first cast. Once the furs have soaked up a little water, the action improves greatly.

Another wonderful thing about flies tied with these materials is that they soak up color like a sponge. Wonderful, realistic baitfish imitations can be created in minutes using a selection of waterproof marking pens. The color does not last forever, but the flies can easily be retouched. If you have no idea what color would be best for a particular trip, leave all the woolheads white. Pack a selection of markers and color them after you've determined what baitfish are in the waters you'll be fishing.

Materials List

HOOK:	Streamer hook, ranging in size from #6 to #4/0.
THREAD:	White 3/0 flat waxed nylon.
BODY:	White lamb's wool (body fur).
TAIL:	Eight to ten strands of clear or pearl-silver flake Sili-legs, with a collar of white arctic fox tail tied over the base of the Sili-legs.
EYES:	Silver-Super Eyes (Magnum), or any hourglass-style eyes; superglue.

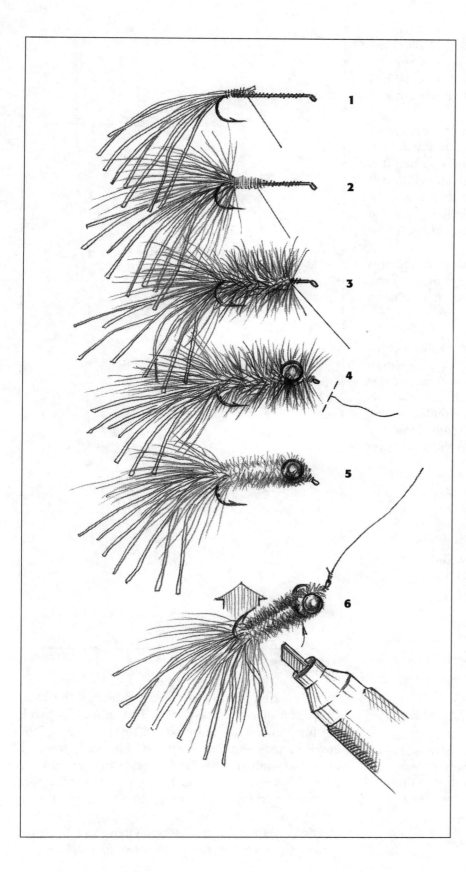

1. Attach the thread, then tie eight to ten strands of Sili-legs onto the rear portion of the hook.

2. Tie a collar of arctic fox tail over the base of the Sili-legs. Remove about half the underfur from this bundle of fur, retaining all the guard hair.

3. Using fine, white lamb's wool, cover about three-quarters of the hook shank. Cut a small bunch of wool from the skin, and remove some of the underfur. Then divide the wool, layering it in different directions. Force the eye of the hook through the bundle of wool, and wrap the thread around the front of the bundle, securing it to the hook. Add more bundles of wool, pressing each bundle tight against the one previously tied to the hook to form the wool body.

4. Tie in the eyes as tight as possible against the wool body. After the eyes are secured, add a drop of superglue to prevent them from twisting when the fly is fished. Cover the space in front of the eyes with more wool, and tie off the thread.

5. Trim the body to the desired shape.

6. Apply color to the fly with the hook point up, since this is the way the streamer swims when retrieved through the water. If you color the fly positioned as it was tied in the vise, this wonderful baitfish imitation will spend all its time swimming upside down.

Baby Crayfish

Over the years, I've designed dozens of flies that looked just great clamped in the jaws of my fly-tying vise. However, soon after I tied these creations onto a tippet and presented them to fish, it was obvious that many of them were terrible.

I now attempt to think "wet," when creating a new wet-fly pattern. I try to envision how the fly will look after it is submerged and how it will move when it is retrieved. After I complete a new wet-fly design, I tie it onto a length of monofilament and take it for a swim in a test tank. If the new pattern doesn't look good in the tank, it won't be presented to the fish or to my fellow fly fishers.

A fair number of my creations have passed this test, but few have shown more promise than the Baby Crayfish. I tried several materials while attempting to imitate the claws on this small crayfish, and all failed. Finally, I made the claws out of a length of soft fur and a little color. Still unimpressed with this newest design when it came off the vise, I attached a length of leader material and took it for a swim. I was thrilled. Seconds after the pattern hit the water, it turned into the real thing. It looked wonderful wet, and the action was superb. This pattern has become one of my favorites, particularly when I'm fishing for stream smallmouths.

Materials List

HOOK:	Mustad 9671, #8 wet nymph hook.
THREAD:	Black or dark brown 6/0 waxed.
LEAD WIRE:	#30, tied onto both sides of the hook shank.
SMALL LEGS:	Brown grizzly hackle.
BODY:	Any long-fiber, dark brown fur.
ANTENNAE:	Any long, coarse, dark brown hair.
MOUTH:	Fine, dark brown deer tail and orange hackle.
EYES:	#3 black bead chain (available at craft stores).
CLAWS:	Any soft, cream-colored wool or wool-like fur. Dyed sheep, raccoon, coyote, and arctic fox work well. Remove the guard hairs before tying in the claws.
WATERPROOF MARKER:	Any reddish brown color.
SUPERGLUE:	Used to secure the lead wire.

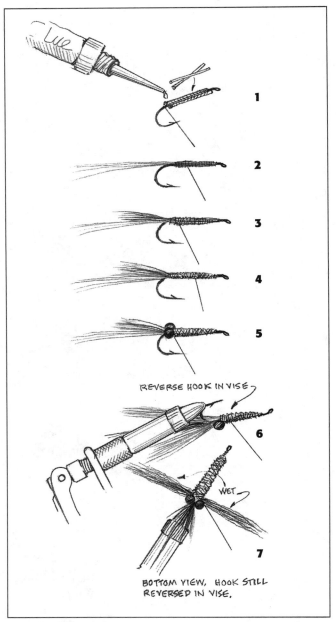

1

2

3

4

5

REVERSE HOOK IN VISE

6

WET

7

BOTTOM VIEW, HOOK STILL
REVERSED IN VISE.

FIRST DRAWING

🐜 Compared with most crayfish patterns, the Baby Crayfish is quick and easy to tie. The only tricky part is the fur claws. The claws extend from the top of the crayfish, just behind the eyes, but it is nearly impossible to position and tie the fur inside the gap of a #8 hook. I found that it is much easier to tie the fur onto the front portion of the body, then wrap the thread back toward the back of the hook, inching the fur into position. Wetting the fur before dividing and X-ing the claws also makes it easier to complete them.

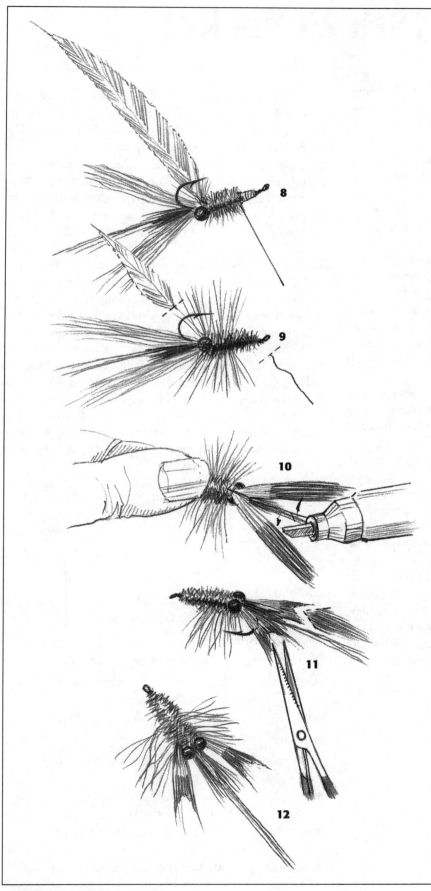

FIRST DRAWING

1. Attach the thread, then tie in a length of lead wire onto the front side of the hook shank. Tie another piece of lead wire to the other side of the hook shank, then apply a couple drops of superglue to secure the lead.

2. Tie in six to eight strands of hair to form the antennae, extending the material a full hook length beyond the rear of the hook.

3. Attach a small amount of fine, dark brown deer tail on top of the antennae. The hair should extend about half the length of the antennae.

4. Tie six to eight bright orange hackle barbs over the top of the deer hair.

5. Attach a pair of black bead-chain eyes. Use metal eyes. *Do not use plastic.*

6. Rotate the fly (hook point up), and tie the fur claws onto the top of the hook shank. Make the first few wraps, then wrap the thread back toward the eyes. Continue to inch the thread back until the fur is secured at the base of the eyes.

7. Divide the fur, then X the base with a few wraps of thread to separate the claws. Wetting the fur with a little water makes this step much easier.

SECOND DRAWING

8. Attach a brown grizzly hackle, then dub about two-thirds of the body with any long-fiber, dark brown fur.

9. Palmer-tie the hackle forward (three turns), and tie it off. Remove the excess hackle, dub the remaining portion of the body, and tie off the head.

10. After trimming the grizzly hackle from the top and bottom of the crayfish, color the end of the claws with a reddish brown marker.

11. While the ends of the claws are still wet, trim to shape with scissors.

12. The completed crayfish is shown from the top.

T. P. Stickleback

Thirty years of pursuing stream trout has had a strong influence on my fly tying. Even when I'm tying flies that are meant to imitate things other than aquatic insects, I'm very aware of the importance of matching the imitation to the natural. If a well-tied dry fly can convince a wary brown trout that the combination of steel, fur, and feathers that just drifted by is a specific insect, why shouldn't the tier make the same effort to produce a streamer that looks like the real thing?

Through the years, I've tied thousands of streamers. Some of these patterns were made of brightly colored materials, and the final products looked like nothing that ever swam in fresh or salt water. Most of the streamers I've tied and fished were intended to imitate specific baitfish, including shiners, sculpins, dace, smelts, silversides, and even adult herring. But I had never come across a pattern that resembled the small fish spit up by smallmouth bass in the bottom of my boat.

After identifying the small fish as sticklebacks, I tried fishing a few established patterns that looked something like them. I wasn't really surprised when the bass refused them. The overall shape of the conventional streamers just didn't match the extended body shape and tail of the stickleback.

It was this distinctive body shape and tail that created problems when I first attempted to design a stickleback imitation. However, after developing the "toothpick method" for extending the body on these streamers, I successfully fished this pattern in waters containing resident populations of sticklebacks, including one of my favorite lakes in southern Quebec. What surprised me was that this streamer is also very productive in waters that do not contain sticklebacks. I have taken numerous warm-water and cold-water species on this pattern, including some fish that I am sure have never seen a stickleback.

The sticklebacks, members of the family Gasterosteidae, are inhabitants of the North Temperate Zone, with most species found in North America. The brook stickleback is found only in fresh water, while the three-spine and four-spine varieties are common in both fresh and salt water. These little fish are found in many of the waters frequented by anglers and are commonly preyed on by the larger fish we hope to catch, especially during the spring spawning period.

Habits may vary slightly from species to species, but all these little nest builders have interesting courtship and breeding rituals. The male builds the nest, cementing bits of algae or plant detritus together with a substance discharged from his kidneys. Once the nest is completed, the female stickleback is encouraged to enter. She deposits the eggs in the nest and squirms out the other side. The male enters the nest, fertilizes the spawn, then leaves the nest but remains in the area to fan the eggs, keep the nest repaired, and drive off any intruders. As the eggs hatch, the male herds the fry, keeping them around the nest until the new generation becomes too active to retrieve, at which time the male stickleback abandons them.

Materials List

HOOK:	#4 straight-eye streamer.
THREAD:	White 3/0.
EXTENDED BODY:	Section of a round toothpick.
TAIL:	Two partridge or hen pheasant feathers, trimmed to shape.
BODY:	Any coarse, light brown, dubbed fur.
RIBBING:	Silver oval tinsel.
WING:	Matched pair of dyed brown grizzly hackles.
HEAD:	Light brown, trimmed lamb's wool, colored with markers.
EYES:	Very small doll eyes attached with five-minute epoxy.
WATERPROOF MARKERS:	Reddish brown, black, and red.

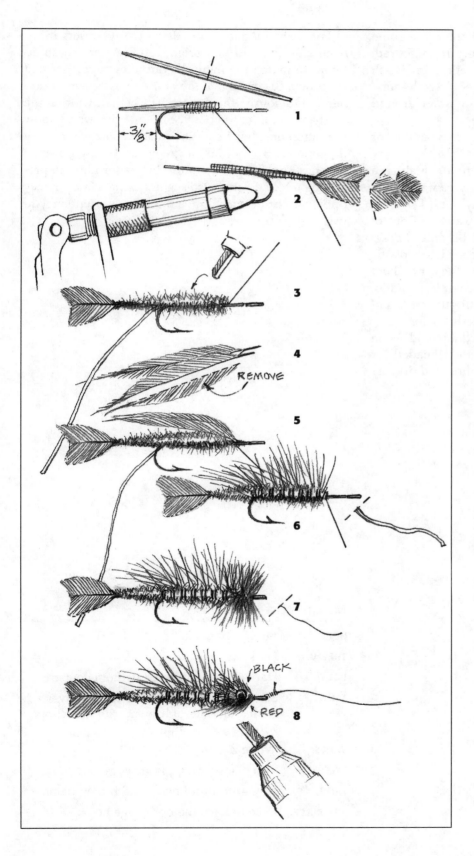

1. Tie a section of a round toothpick onto the top of the hook. The end of the toothpick should extend $3/8$ inch beyond the bend of the hook.

2. Select a matched pair of light brown partridge or hen pheasant feathers. Place the two feathers back to back, and trim them to the desired shape. With the fly reversed in the vise, secure the tail onto either side of the end of the toothpick.

3. Cover the extended portion of the body with light brown dubbing, then return the hook to its normal position in the vise. Tie in the length of silver oval tinsel, and complete the dubbing. Color the top of the body with reddish brown marker.

4. Select a pair of dyed brown grizzly hackles for the wing. Strip away the hackle barbs from the bottom portion of each hackle.

5. Attach the front of the wing with several wraps of thread.

6. Pull the wing back tight along the top of the body, then make the first wrap with the silver rib. Continue wrapping the rib forward, around the body and through the wing, to complete the Matuka-style wing. Tie off and remove the excess rib.

7. Tie in the lamb's wool head, and tie off the thread.

8. Trim the head to shape with scissors. Color the top of the head black and the bottom red. Attach small doll eyes to complete the pattern.

Red Dragonfly

They vary in size and color, but some of the dragonflies I see are bright red. Bass and panfish chase these red varieties. Small fish often jump completely out of the water to catch them. Larger fish splash and move a lot of water around while pursuing these evasive bits of food.

Some insects can easily be caught in your hat or hand, but the flying skills of the dragonfly make it very difficult to capture. One morning, standing in about a foot of water while trying to focus my camera, I felt something crawling up the back of my neck. I swatted it, and something dropped into the water in front of me. To my surprise, it was one of the bright red dragonflies. I carefully picked it up and placed it in a plastic film container. As soon as I got back to the car and out of my waders, I opened up my watercolor box and located a sketch pad. I wanted to capture the details of the specimen before it lost its wonderful color. After completing the color notes, I included a few ideas on how I might tie the imitation, and then headed for home. A couple of hours later, I had three red dragonflies ready for the water.

For years, I had depended on my observations from afar and had tied bright red creations in an attempt to match the naturals. But after capturing that specimen, I learned that the entire fly is brown underneath. Obviously, the pattern can be tied without the red hair on top of the body, since the fish won't know the difference, but I still like to add color when tying dragonflies. Bright blue or green can be used instead of red. Use a little floatant on this pattern before presenting it to the fish. I also suggest using a fairly heavy tippet (4X or heavier), since this fly has a tendency to twist lighter tippets.

Materials List

HOOK:	#8 dry-fly hook.
THREAD:	Dark brown 6/0.
BODY:	Dark brown dubbing (medium-coarse).
TAIL:	Small amount of red deer tail tied over a similar amount of brown, with fine copper wire for segmenting.
WINGS:	White Z-Lon.
EYES:	Two black (bead) plastic eyes.
PAINT:	Any waterproof black and brown paint.
SUPERGLUE:	Used to keep the body together.

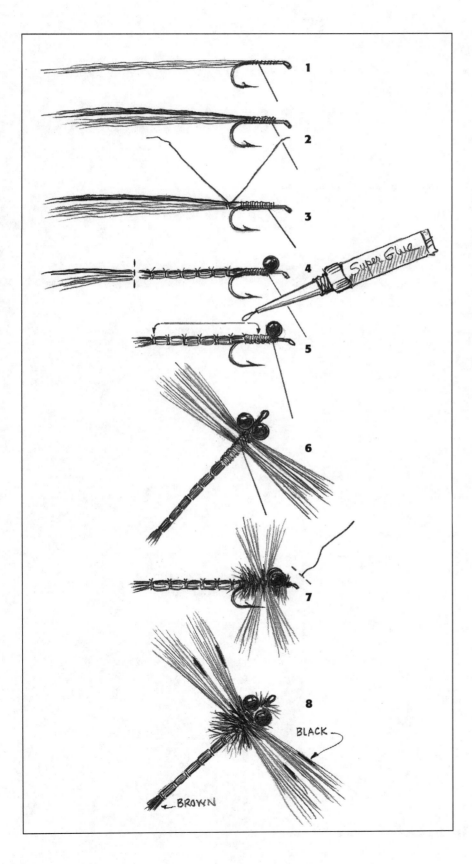

1. Attach the thread, and tie on a small amount of brown deer tail. It should be at least three times the length of the hook shank.

2. Tie in a similar amount of red deer tail over the brown.

3. Begin to segment the body. Position a short length of fine copper wire under the deer hair, cross the wire over the top, pull the wire tight, twist the strands of wire around two or three times, and trim off the excess.

4. Continue until the segments are complete, and remove the excess deer tail. Then tie on a pair of black plastic eyes.

5. After the eyes are secured, apply a little superglue to the body and between the eyes.

6. Tie in the wings. It is much easier if you wet the Z-Lon beforehand.

7. Complete the body using any dark brown dubbing material, and tie off the head. A little of the dubbing may be teased from under the body to simulate legs.

8. Pull the wings tight, apply a little head cement to the wing to stiffen it slightly. Let it dry, then paint a black spot on the leading edge of each wing. The top of the last segment can be colored using a little brown paint.

Nymphs

Bead-Chain Nymph

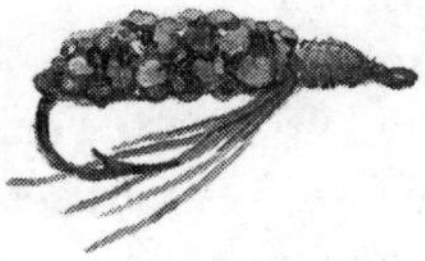

Stone Caddis

Plastic Canvas Stonefly

Bead-Chain Nymph

Most fly fishers prefer trout over panfish, but they welcome any species that will take a fly and put a bend in a light fly rod, especially during the early season, when the trout streams are still high and ice cold.

One afternoon, I returned from my favorite warm-water pond and inventoried my stock of flies. It was time to replenish the supply. I sat down to tie a few panfish flies and found that my work area was a mess. There were bits of feathers and clumps of dubbing fur scattered everywhere. I pushed the remnants of my past efforts to the side and tied up a couple dozen panfish flies. Then I set out to clean up the tying bench. I was about to throw out the bits of hackle and dubbing fur, but I decided instead to experiment with these leftover materials, possibly putting them to good use.

I secured a hook in the jaws of the vise and tied a pair of bead-chain eyes onto the front of the straight portion of the hook. Rather than tying on a clump of rabbit fur, I tied on a more traditional tail using some of the fibers taken from a section of a brown hackle feather. I found a length of gold oval tinsel under the pile of feathers and fur. It was a bit short, but if I used the hackle pliers to hold the piece, it would serve as the rib. I tied it onto the hook, used some of the discarded dubbing to cover the rear portion of the hook shank, then wrapped the tinsel forward to form the rib and tied it off.

At this point, I almost continued with the steps required to complete a conventional nymph. However, because the bead chain was heavy enough to turn the fly hook point up, I rotated it 180 degrees in the vise and attempted to tie in a section of turkey feather that would later form the wing pad. This proved to be a pain in the neck. The bend of the hook and the point were in the way. Finally, I unwrapped the thread and gave up on using the section of turkey feather. I found a length of small mylar piping in all the mess, bent it in half, and tied it onto the top of the fly just behind the eyes. The piping was much easier to handle than the feather, and with any luck, it would form a decent-looking wing pad after I pulled it forward over the thorax. I covered the remaining portion of the hook shank with more dubbing, completing the thorax. I pulled the piping forward and secured it just behind the eye, then removed the excess piping and tied off the head. Finally, to complete the pattern, I picked out a little of the dubbing fur from behind the eyes to form the legs.

I have made only one addition to these nymphs since tying the prototype. I now coat the top of the wing pad with a little epoxy. This produces an opal-like appearance in the wing pad, which the trout seem to like. The majority of Bead-Chain Nymphs I've made in recent years have been tied in a variety of colors rather than any specific pattern. I tie several different sizes with cream, dun, brown, and black dubbing. This style of nymph isn't as fancy as some, but it does a better job of getting down into those deep, dark pools, and it rarely hangs up, since it rides hook point up. I have taken trout on Bead-Chain Nymphs when the fish wouldn't look at traditional nymph patterns.

Faux Fur is an acrylic fur that the manufacturer advertises as being "perfect to trim Santa outfits, make fur hats, capes, boots, accessories, and animals." When I called the company to locate a source of supply, I suggested that it add "excellent dubbing for a variety of trout flies" to the list of uses for this product. I've purchased dozens of different synthetic furs, and few, if any, have proved to be worth a darn when I attempted to spin the material around a thread, then around the shank of a hook. Faux Fur comes in a variety of wonderful "buggy-looking" colors. A couple of dollars worth will tie hundreds of flies. This synthetic fur can be purchased in many craft stores, fabric stores, and chain stores throughout the country. If you are unable to find Faux Fur in a store near you, contact Kirchen Brothers, Box 1016, Skokie, IL 60076.

Materials List

HOOK:	#8, #10, or #12 traditional 2XL nymph hook.
THREAD:	Light brown 6/0 or 8/0.
BODY:	Brown Faux Fur, with the guard hairs removed.
TAIL:	About a dozen brown hackle fibers.
RIB:	Fine gold oval tinsel.
WING PAD:	Small mylar piping (pearl).
THORAX:	Brown Faux Fur, with the guard hairs.
LEGS:	Strands of hair picked out of each side of the thorax with a bodkin.
EYES:	Standard-size black bead chain.
FIVE-MINUTE EPOXY:	Used to coat the wing pad.

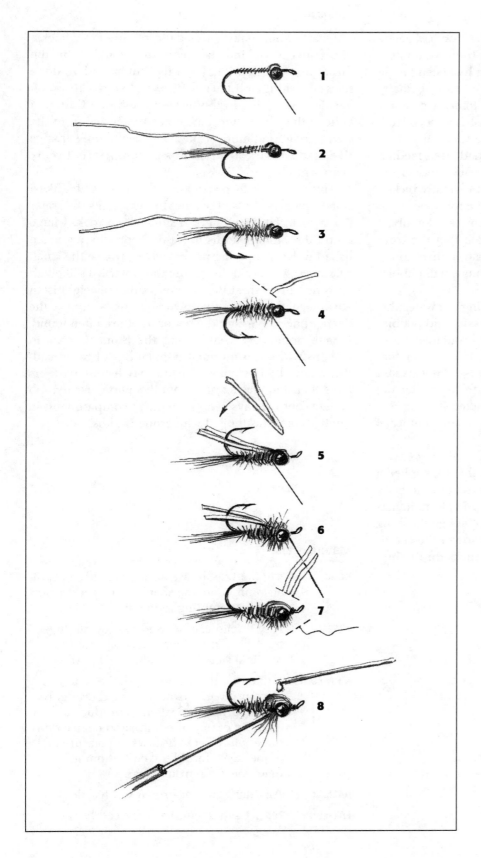

1. Cover the hook shank with thread, attach the bead-chain eyes, and add a drop of head cement.

2. Tie on the tail, then tie in a length of fine gold oval tinsel.

3. Cover the body with Faux Fur dubbing (guard hairs removed).

4. Wrap the tinsel forward to produce the rib, and tie it off.

5. Rotate the fly in the vise. Cut a short length of piping, then bend it and tie it on top of the body, just behind the eyes.

6. Using Faux Fur (include the guard hairs), tie in the thorax. Be sure to X some of the dubbing between the eyes.

7. Pull the mylar piping forward, and tie it off just behind the eye of the hook. Remove the excess piping, and finish off the head of the fly.

8. Pick out a little fur from either side of the thorax to form the legs, then coat the top of the wing pad with a little epoxy to complete the fly.

Stone Caddis

I was trying to catch a few fish for supper. We had guests arriving from out of town, and fresh trout would be a treat for these city folks, but the fishing had been tough. After nearly an hour of pounding the water, I finally took the first fish. Hoping that the stomach contents would offer some clue as to what the fish had been feeding on, I cleaned the fish and saved the stomach.

The stomach was full, so the fish had been feeding on something. I opened it with my knife, and to my surprise, it was full of small pebbles. I carefully picked through the contents, searching for some clue as to why this trout had been feeding on rocks. Finally, I found an intact clump and discovered that the trout had been feeding on caddis larvae, eating them along with the cases the insects had built using small pebbles from the bottom of the stream.

This triggered an idea. Before leaving the water that morning, I collected some of the fine sand and pebbles from the bottom of the stream, filling a container I normally use when collecting insect samples. Later that week, I rinsed the material to remove any debris and spread it out in a shallow container to dry. After the sand and pebble mixture was dry, I sifted it using several different wire sieves to produce a small quantity of fine, medium, and coarse material.

Making up a supply of the Stone Caddis was easy. I simply prewrapped a few hooks with thread, applied a little five-minute epoxy to the rear portion of the hook shank, and set the hook into a small pile of the material. As the epoxy began to harden, I removed the hook and kneaded the material into the shape of the caddis cases I'd seen clinging to the larger rocks on the bottom of the stream.

I started out making this pattern with a few hackle barbs tied in behind the head, like you'd tie in the throat on a conventional wet fly. But since I've done so well fishing soft-hackle flies, I changed to a soft hackle when tying in the legs on the Stone Caddis. I believe that the softer hackle has better action in the water, triggering more strikes. This is the only change I've made since I first tied this pattern nearly twenty years ago.

This particular fly doesn't exactly hit the water like a small, sparsely dressed dry fly. In fact, it hits the water like a rock. However, it also sinks like a rock. I have found the Stone Caddis to be most productive when fished in faster-moving pocket water, where the small splash caused by the fly hitting the water isn't likely to present a problem. Once in the water, its weight is an advantage, getting the fly down near the bottom of the deeper pockets, where the better trout are often found. I have done very well fishing the Stone Caddis in streams with even minimal populations of cased caddis, especially in smaller streams. My fishing partners have their fun teasing me about this particular nymph pattern, but I always keep a couple of compartments in my fly box well supplied with Stone Caddis.

Materials List

HOOK: #8 to #12. Choose a shank length that will accommodate the shape of the caddis case you're attempting to imitate.

THREAD: Any thread can be used to prewrap the hook shank. Light green 3/0 is used for the final steps and for the head of the fly.

BODY MATERIAL: Fine sand collected from the bottom of your favorite trout stream, thoroughly rinsed, dried, and sifted to produce a quantity of fine, medium, and coarse body material. (Check the laws in your area. Some states forbid the collection of materials from trout streams.)

HACKLE: Any dark gray or brown soft hackle.

FIVE-MINUTE EPOXY: Used to construct the caddis cases.

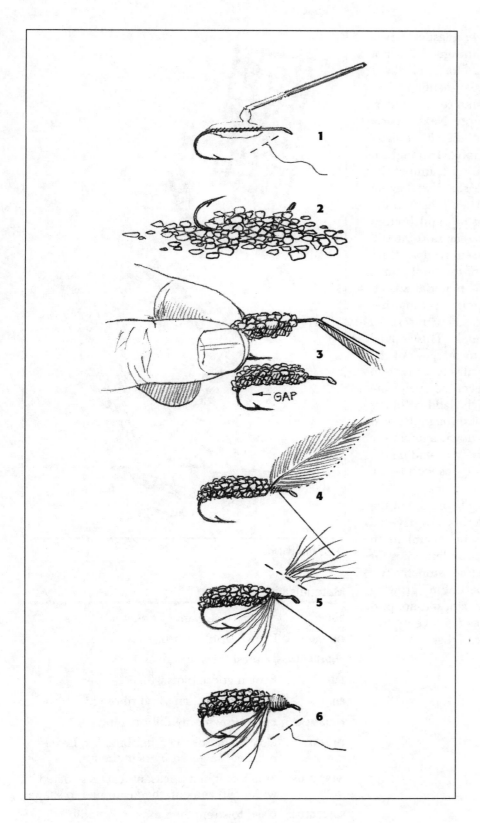

1. Prewrap the hook shank with thread, then tie off. Apply the five-minute epoxy to the rear portion of the hook shank.

2. Place the fly in the sand and cover it. Let it set until the epoxy begins to thicken.

3. Remove the fly from the sand, and shape the caddis case with your fingers. Be careful not to close up the hook gap. Keep the majority of the material on the top of the hook. Wetting your fingers with a little soapy water allows you to shape the fly without having your fingers stick to it.

4. After the epoxy has hardened, reattach the thread and tie in the soft hackle.

5. Wrap in two turns of the hackle, tie it off, and remove the excess from the top of the fly.

6. Wrap the head, shaping as you go, then tie off the thread and add a drop of head cement.

Plastic Canvas Stonefly

For several years, I pondered over plastic canvas whenever I visited a craft store, intrigued but not convinced that I could find a good use for it. Finally, I purchased a sheet of it and began experimenting.

I cut and tied pieces of the stuff onto several different hooks, rejecting these first attempts. Next, I cut a narrow, ladderlike strip off the edge of the plastic sheet and held it against the top of the hook. I thought it might be used to form an underbody. I trimmed the strip to match the length of the hook shank and again held it against the top of the hook. Then I tapered the strip at both ends by removing the top and bottom rungs of the ladderlike piece. The rear portion still needed a bit more tapering, so I removed another rung. I tied the piece onto the top of the hook, but I wasn't happy with the area where the material was attached to the hook—too big of a bump. I cut another piece and tapered the ends of the plastic with scissors and tied this piece onto another hook. This looked much better. I put another hook into the jaws of the vise and trimmed a piece of the plastic canvas to shape. As I started to attach this piece, the eye of the hook ended up between the rungs of the ladder. Rather than removing the piece, I threaded it through the next rung. Next, I forced the two ends down against the hook shank. The underbody formed by threading the hook through the rungs of the ladder was wonderful. Finally, I had found a use for plastic canvas.

Plastic canvas comes in a variety of colors, but the color isn't important, since the underbody is covered with other materials. It also comes in several mesh sizes, making it possible to construct underbodies for smaller mayfly nymphs, as well as larger stonefly creations. This craft store item is now part of my growing inventory of fly-tying stuff. I recently stocked up, purchasing three sheets of plastic canvas for seventy-five cents. That's enough to tie thousands of flies.

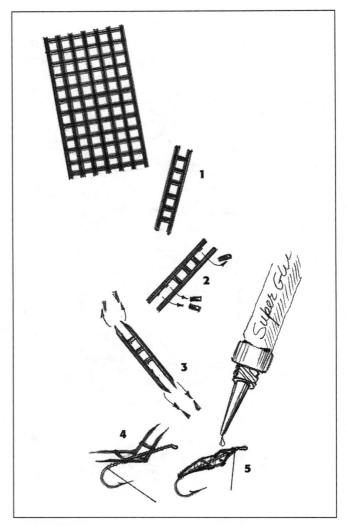

FIRST DRAWING

Materials List

HOOK:	#6 or #8 streamer hook.
THREAD:	Brown or black 6/0.
UNDERBODY:	#7 mesh plastic canvas.
TAIL:	Brown goose biots.
RIB:	Small, round, tan vinyl ribbing.
ABDOMEN:	Fine, brown poly dubbing fur.
THORAX:	Coarse, dark brown dubbing fur. Leave most of the guard hairs in the fur.
WING PADS:	Small, soft hen pheasant feathers coated with head cement, then trimmed to shape.
SUPERGLUE:	Used to strengthen the underbody.

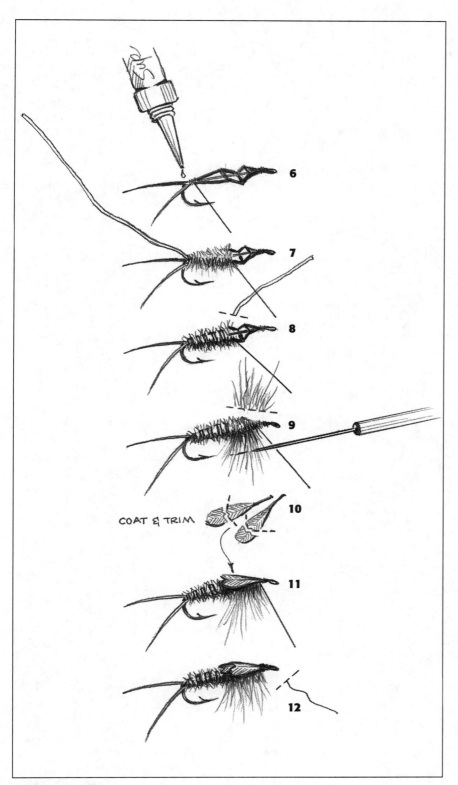

SECOND DRAWING

FIRST DRAWING

1. Cut a narrow, ladderlike strip with six rungs from a sheet of plastic canvas.

2. Remove two rungs from the bottom of the ladder and one rung from the top.

3. Taper the ends of the plastic.

4. Prewrap the hook shank with thread, then thread the ladder onto the hook.

5. Tie both ends of the piece securely to the shank of the hook, then tie off the thread. A generous amount of superglue strengthens the underbody and prevents it from twisting on the hook.

SECOND DRAWING

6. After the superglue has hardened, return the thread to the rear of the plastic canvas underbody and tie in the tails. Apply a tiny drop of superglue to the base of the tails to keep them in position.

7. Tie in the small, round vinyl ribbing. Then cover the rear portion of the body with fine, brown dubbing fur.

8. Wrap the rib forward through the dubbing, tie it off, and remove the excess.

9. Cover the thorax with coarse dubbing (include some of the guard hairs). Pick out some of the underfur and guard hairs with a bodkin, then trim the excess off the top of the thorax.

10. Pick out two small soft hackles (hen pheasant or grouse). Coat the hackles with head cement, and work the cement into them by pulling them between your fingers. Let them dry, then trim to shape.

11. Tie one of the hackles over the top of the thorax. The end of the hackle (wing pad) should run about halfway along the top of the body.

12. Attach the second hackle, positioning it slightly forward of the first, and tie off the thread.

Poppers

Mini-Popper

Single-Fold Popper

Lipped Popper

Pencil Sharpener Popper

Mini-Popper

If I'd been fishing for trout, I would have matched the hatch, tying on a #14 cream-colored Elk Hair Caddis. However, all the flies I had with me were intended for panfish and bass, not trout. Everyone knows that panfish aren't that selective. Any old thing dropped onto the water triggers an instant response.

I started out with a popper tied on a #10 hook and presented it to the feeding fish. The fish continued to take the naturals, but very few showed any interest in my popper. I changed colors several times, but that didn't help much. The problem was that the popper was too big. It should have been about half the size. I didn't have any poppers close to the size of the flies the fish were taking that particular evening, but I vowed to solve that problem before returning to the pond.

The next morning, I attempted to tie a supply of smaller poppers. After trying to make the tiny bodies with a variety of materials, I determined that it was time to make a trip to the craft store. The 3/16-inch-square lengths of balsa wood were forty-nine cents each. I purchased two, supplying me with enough material to make hundreds of the smaller poppers.

After shaping a tiny balsa wood body, I decided to put a small groove in the bottom of it to accommodate the hook shank. This attempt failed. The grooved bodies broke when I tried to tie them onto the hook. Finally, I attached the thread to the hook, made up another body without the groove, held it on top of the hook, made ten or twelve wraps around the balsa wood, and tied off the thread. The wraps of thread held the body in place long enough for me to coat it with five-minute epoxy. After painting the body, dabbing on a little color for the eyes, and tying in the tail, the next step was to see if the popper was durable enough to catch a fair number of panfish before it was destroyed.

That same afternoon, the caddisflies and I were both back on the water. Armed with a supply of my new Mini-Poppers, I chose one tied on a #14 dry-fly hook and presented it to the feeding fish. On the very first cast, a fish took the tiny offering. Expecting a small fish, I raised the rod and tried to retrieve the line. The fish had other plans, doubling the light rod. After a short, fierce battle, I brought the fish to the net. I took a moment to admire the large crappie, then unhooked it and returned it to the water.

The strikes came easily. Rarely did I have to make more than a couple of casts before a fish took one of the Mini-Poppers. However, as is often the case with my new creations, the tiny poppers required one small change. The bluegills had the bad habit of taking the small poppers down to their tails, making it difficult to remove the poppers from their small mouths. However, turning down the barb with hemostats eliminated the problem.

I caught several dozen fish on that first tiny popper, then fished some of the others that afternoon. All the Mini-Poppers held up very well. In fact, after returning home, I gave them a closer look. If the poppers I had fished hadn't still been wet, I couldn't have distinguished them from the unused ones. Coating the tiny piece of balsa wood with epoxy had resulted in a very durable, very productive popper.

Materials List

HOOK:	#12 to #16 dry-fly hook; barbless, or pinch down the barb.
THREAD:	Any color 3/0 waxed to attach the body; 6/0 to tie on the hackle and tail.
BODY:	Strips of 3/16-inch-square balsa wood lengths.
TAIL:	Your choice of materials.
SANDPAPER POINTER:	Used to shape the body.
FIVE-MINUTE EPOXY:	Used to secure the body to the hook and seal the wood.
PAINT:	Fingernail polish works well.

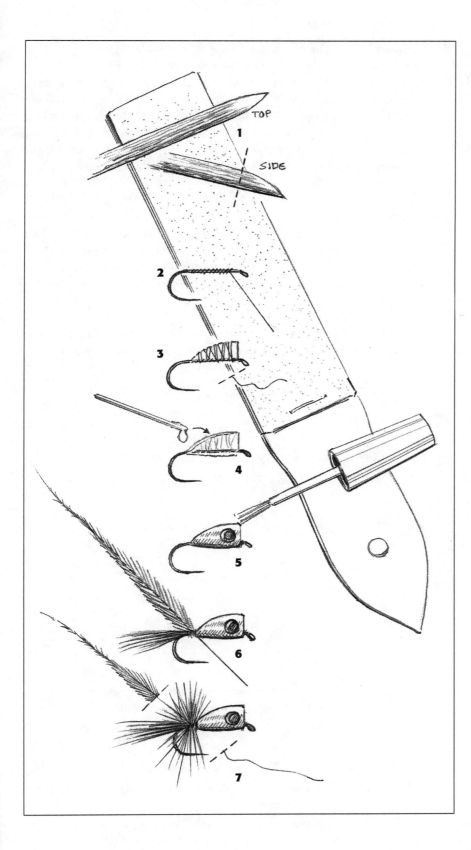

1. Shape the sides and top of the end of a 3/16-inch balsa wood piece, leaving the bottom flat. Then cut the body to the desired length with a sharp knife. A sandpaper pointer works well when shaping the wooden popper bodies. Artists use this small, inexpensive device to sharpen the points on pencils. It can be found at art supply stores.

2. Attach the 3/0 flat waxed thread to the hook.

3. Position the balsa wood body on top of the hook shank and make ten to twelve wraps. Use a fair amount of pressure, but not enough to crush the soft wood, and tie off.

4. Adjust the hook so that it is aligned with the popper body, then coat the entire body with five-minute epoxy. Turn the popper in the vise, or put it on a drying wheel, until the epoxy has hardened.

5. Paint the body and eyes. The body can be any color, but I recommend that the face of the popper body be painted white or some other light color, so that you can easily see the popper when it is fished.

6. Reattach the thread. Use 6/0 to attach the tail and hackle.

7. Make several wraps with the hackle, then tie off the thread. Add a drop of head cement to the rear of the body to secure the thread, completing the popper.

Single-Fold Popper

The head of this popper is made from a sheet of foam commonly found at craft stores. The sheets are 9 by 12 inches and 4 millimeters thick (about 1/4 inch). The foam comes in a variety of colors and costs about a dollar per sheet. A single sheet will make over 100 poppers.

I use a plastic worm hook when making this popper, because the unique bend in the shank acts as a stop when the foam is folded and pushed forward on the hook shank. The bend in the hook shank also positions the eye at the bottom of the head, improving the splash when the popper is retrieved.

The Single-Fold Popper body is simple to make, and the finished product looks great, if the foam is cut carefully. Take your time, and mark the width of each strip with a fine-tip marker. Use a straightedge and an X-acto knife to cut the foam into strips. Stack four or five of the strips flat on the cutting surface, then mark the desired length on the top and the bottom of the strips. Line them up against the side of the straightedge, and cut the strips to length, as square as possible. After you have cut the foam pieces to the desired size, mark the center of each piece. The easiest way to do this is to draw lines crisscrossing from corner to corner. The center of the piece is where the lines intersect.

Start out with the size indicated, then experiment with different widths and lengths. Just remember to cut the pieces carefully, so that the sides and face of the popper head line up when they are glued together. After you have made several bodies, have fun completing the poppers with the materials of your choice.

Materials List

HOOK:	#1/0 or #2/0 plastic worm hook.
THREAD:	3/0 to match the color of the foam.
HEAD:	4-mm sheet foam.
TAIL:	Your choice of materials.
DOLL EYES:	Your choice, attached with five-minute epoxy.
SUPERGLUE:	Used to secure the head.

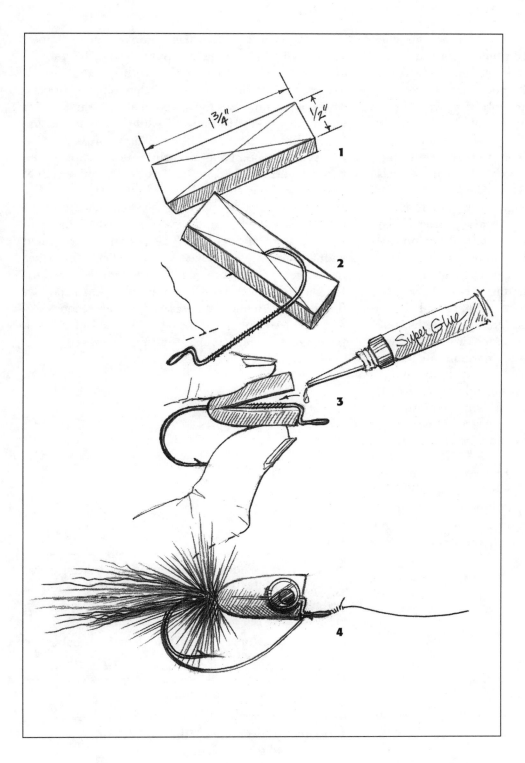

1. Cut the foam to the desired size, and mark the center of the piece.

2. Prewrap the shank of the hook with thread, then push the point of the hook through the center of the foam piece.

3. Bend the foam, and slide the piece forward until it is tight against the bend in the hook shank. Apply a little superglue to both surfaces of the foam and the thread, then press the top and bottom sections of the foam together and hold until the glue sets. Check the face of the popper to make sure the eye of the hook is lined up properly before the superglue is dry.

4. Attach a pair of doll eyes with five-minute epoxy. After the epoxy has hardened, the tail of the popper can be completed with a variety of materials. Use whatever is available. A monofilament weedguard is also a good idea, particularly when you're fishing for largemouth bass.

Lipped Popper

Attaching the body to the hook is a basic step when making a popper, but even the basics can be improved. For many years, I depended on epoxy to secure the body to the hook, but I discovered that superglue does a much better job of preventing the body from twisting on the hook shank. While attempting to scrape several layers of superglue off a bodkin, I noticed that it seemed to adhere to metal better than epoxy did. A simple test proved it. I glued two balsa wood bodies to standard hooks (not kink-shank hooks). I used epoxy on one, superglue on the other, and let them dry overnight. The next morning, I tested them. It took a little effort, but I was able to twist the body attached with the epoxy around the hook shank. The superglued body was much stronger. I actually broke the balsa wood body while attempting to twist it.

I also learned how to make poppers with better-looking, more durable bodies. After the body has been trimmed to shape and finish-sanded, it is coated with five-minute epoxy. As the epoxy hardens, air bubbles usually form in the surface. You can easily remove these imperfections just before the epoxy hardens. Wet your finger in a little soapy water, then gently run your finger back and forth over the surface of the popper body. This simple trick removes the imperfections, resulting in a smooth body.

When you paint the popper body is also important. If you let the epoxy set until it has completely cured and then paint the body, the paint sometimes chips off. If you apply a coat of paint after the epoxy has begun to harden but is still a little sticky to the touch, the paint adheres much better.

These days, I seldom fish a conventional popper. While trying to improve the appearance and durability of my poppers, I also came up with a better design. Several seasons back, I made up a few Lipped Poppers. This popper simulates the action of a struggling baitfish when it is retrieved. It takes a while to cut and attach the lip, but it is time well spent. The improved action makes the Lipped Popper much more attractive to the fish, triggering explosive strikes when conventional poppers are refused.

After the Lipped Popper hits the water, let it rest for a few seconds, then point the rod tip directly at the popper and begin the retrieve. This pattern is best fished with a "stop-strip" retrieve. A short, quick strip makes the popper wiggle from side to side and dive slightly. Longer, slower strips of a foot or more make the popper dive, then swim under the surface for a few seconds. Alternate the stripping methods to make the Lipped Popper simulate the action of a struggling minnow.

Materials List

HOOK:	Any hook that accommodates the size of the body and the fish.
THREAD:	3/0 flat waxed. Match the color to that of the materials used for the tail.
BODY:	3/8- or 1/2-inch-square lengths of balsa wood.
POPPER LIP:	Cut from the top, bottom, or sides of plastic hook boxes.
TAIL:	Your choice of materials.
SUPERGLUE:	Used to attach the balsa wood body to the hook shank.
FIVE-MINUTE EPOXY:	Used to coat the body and to secure the lip to the body.
PAINT:	Fingernail polish works well. Also used for the eyes.

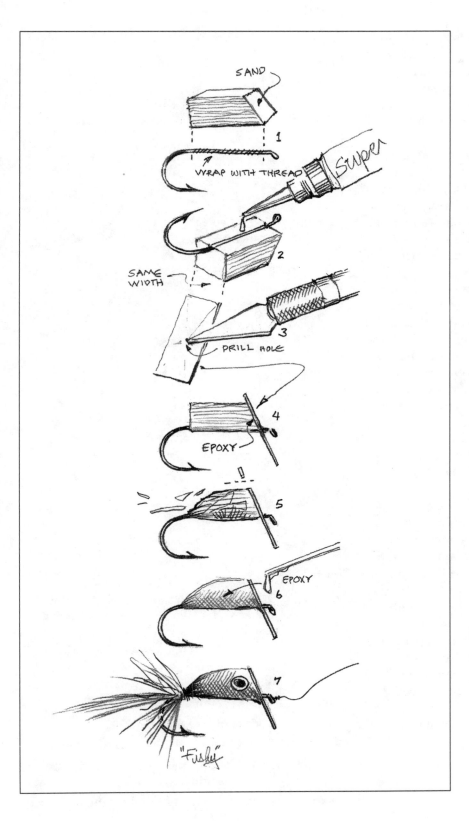

1. Prewrap the hook shank with thread, covering only the area where the body will be glued to the hook, and tie off. Cut the end of the balsa wood off at an angle (about 45 degrees), and sand the face smooth. Next, measure the area of the hook shank that was covered with thread to establish the body length, and cut the body to size.

2. Using a short piece of a hacksaw blade, cut a shallow groove into the bottom of the body. Force the hook into the groove, apply superglue along the entire length of the opening, and set it aside to dry.

3. Cut a piece from a clear plastic hook box that is the width of the balsa wood ($3/8$-inch stock was used in the drawing) and about 1 inch long. Stick the point of an X-acto knife into the center of the piece, then push and twist the blade to drill a hole large enough to push the eye of the hook through it.

4. Push the eye of the hook through the hole in the plastic lip. Apply a little five-minute epoxy to the face of the body, then position the lip and set it aside to harden.

5. Remove the excess plastic lip from the top of the fly. Fingernail clippers work well for this task. Start shaping the body, using an X-acto knife.

6. Finish shaping the body with a sandpaper pointer (see the pointer shown in the Mini-Popper drawing), then apply a coat of five-minute epoxy to the body (not the face). Turn the fly in the vise until the epoxy thickens, then smooth the surface with your finger. Use enough epoxy so that it fills the groove in the bottom of the body. I apply a little more epoxy on the bottom of the body to add some weight. This helps the fly turn upright when it hits the water.

7. Paint the body and face with fingernail polish, and paint on the eyes. Tie on the tail. Then, using nail clippers, trim the bottom of the plastic lip to complete the pattern.

Pencil Sharpener Popper

I make up dozens of Mini-Poppers and larger bass poppers and present them to panfish and bass throughout the season. But I also fish the Pencil Sharpener Popper. The Pencil Sharpener Popper is a bit larger and longer than the Mini-Popper and smaller than the majority of my bass poppers, so it triggers strikes from both panfish and bass.

The Pencil Sharpener Popper is quick and easy to make. It takes only a few minutes to make up a dozen bodies. First, the end of a balsa wood stick is sharpened in an electric pencil sharpener. A hand sharpener can be used, but the end of the stick will require a bit more sanding. I use an emery board to finish-sand the pointed end of the balsa wood. Then the popper body is cut to length using a small X-acto saw.

The thread is attached, and the popper body is positioned on top of the hook. The thread is wrapped around the body, working forward to the front of the balsa wood. Then the thread is wrapped back all the way to the pointed end of the body and tied off. As you wrap the thread back toward the end of the body, *increase the pressure*. This bends the balsa wood, securing the rear portion of the body tight against the top of the hook.

After the body has been attached to the hook, I apply a little superglue along the bottom of the body. Once the glue has dried, the body is coated with five-minute epoxy and put on the drying wheel to turn until the epoxy hardens. Remember to use the wet-finger technique to remove the imperfections in the surface of the epoxy, as described in the section on the Lipped Popper. A little paint finishes the body and the eyes, and tying in the tail completes the Pencil Sharpener Popper.

Some of these poppers are tied on hooks with extended shanks, but I generally tie them on #4, #6, and #8 streamer hooks. A Pencil Sharpener Popper made from a 3/16-inch balsa wood stick and a #8 streamer hook will be about 1 1/2 inches long from the eye of the hook to the end of the tail. If you start out with 1/4-inch balsa wood and attach the body to a #4 extended-shank hook, the finished popper will be nearly 3 inches long.

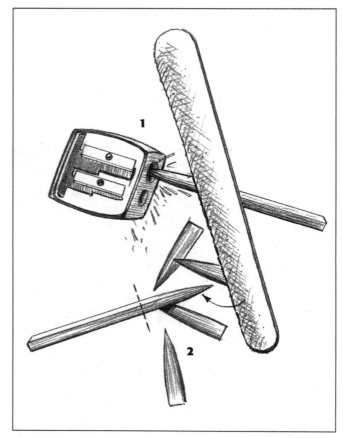

FIRST DRAWING

Materials List

HOOK:	#4, #6, or #8 streamer hook. Streamer hooks with extended hook shanks may also be used.
THREAD:	Any color 3/0 flat waxed nylon, used to attach the body, 6/0 to tie on the hackle and tail.
BODY:	3/16- or 1/4-inch balsa wood sticks.
TAIL:	Your choice of materials.
SUPERGLUE:	Used to secure the body to the hook.
FIVE-MINUTE EPOXY:	Used to coat the body of the popper before painting.
PAINT:	Fingernail polish is used for the body and the eyes.

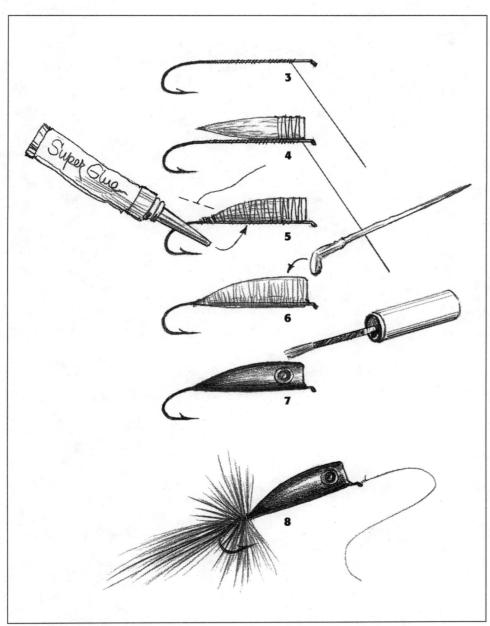

SECOND DRAWING

FIRST DRAWING

1. Form a point at the end of the balsa wood using a pencil sharpener.

2. Finish-sand the point with an emery board, then cut the body to length.

SECOND DRAWING

3. Attach the thread.

4. Position the body on top of the hook, and tie down the front of the popper body.

5. Wrap the thread back toward the pointed end of the body. *Increase* the pressure on the thread as you wrap. This bends the soft balsa wood down against the top of the hook. After you have tied down the point, tie off the thread. A drop or two of superglue applied along the bottom of the body will prevent the body from twisting on the hook when it is fished.

6. Coat the body with five-minute epoxy, and turn it on a drying wheel or in a vise until the epoxy has hardened.

7. Paint the body and the eyes using fingernail polish.

8. Tie in the tail to complete the Pencil Sharpener Popper.

Saltwater Creations

Bead-Chain Crab

Piping Squid

Soda Straw Shrimp

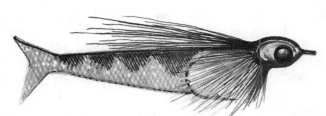

Tuff Tail Streamer

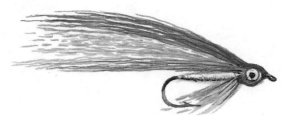

Krystal Flash Fly

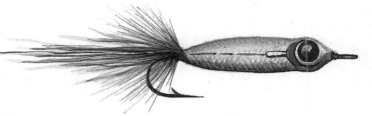

Fishy's Floater

Silversides Streamer

Shad Fly

Bead-Chain Crab

I tie bead-chain eyes on Crazy Charlies, my shad patterns, Bead-Chain Nymphs, and many of the smaller streamers I fish. The additional weight of these metal eyes enables the fly to be fished deeper and greatly improves the action as it is retrieved through the water. The added weight of the bead chain also turns the hook point up. This prevents the fly from snagging when it is fished along the bottom or close to cover, where the fish are most often found.

Since I tie so many flies with these beady eyes, I purchase bead chain by the yard from the local hardware store. After purchasing a supply of the chain, I cut most of it into hundreds of pairs, but I always save a yard or two to experiment with at the vise, hoping to develop new patterns. I have tied pieces of chain along the top of the hook shank and along either side of the hook. I even tried to concoct a tandem fly using bead chain as the link between the two hooks, but none of these attempts worked out very well.

One time, I happened to tie a short length of chain onto the rear portion of a hook. While sitting there trying to decide what to do next, I bent the chain around the back of the hook toward the eye. To my surprise, the chain stiffened as it was bent, forming a rigid crescent shape. I advanced the thread, pulled the end of the chain closer to the eye of the hook, attached it to the front of the hook, and tied off the thread. I placed the combination of metal and thread onto the base of my vise. The instant I saw it, I knew that I'd solved a problem I had been working on since my last trip to the flats.

Many excellent crab patterns have been developed in the past few years, and most will be taken if a fish is willing to eat. However, these patterns are too complicated, very time-consuming to tie, and too large. Many of the things I see scampering along the bottom are closer to a #6, not the "big enough to eat" crabs I see being tied.

The Bead-Chain Crab is easy to tie and is just as productive as many of the crab patterns requiring twice the time, material, and effort to complete. It casts as well as any weighted fly, rarely tangles, and turns right side up seconds after it hits the water. The rather long legs put life into this pattern as it drops or is inched along the bottom, coaxing fish that feed on crabs into inhaling it.

Materials List

HOOK:	#6 standard saltwater hook.
THREAD:	White 3/0.
BODY SUPPORT:	Made from six links of brass bead chain.
LEGS:	Sili-legs (sparkle, tan, or white).
BODY COATING:	E-Z Shape Sparkle Body (sand crab and white).
PAINT:	Pink and black fingernail polish to color the mouth and eyes.
SUPERGLUE:	Used to prevent the body from turning on the hook.

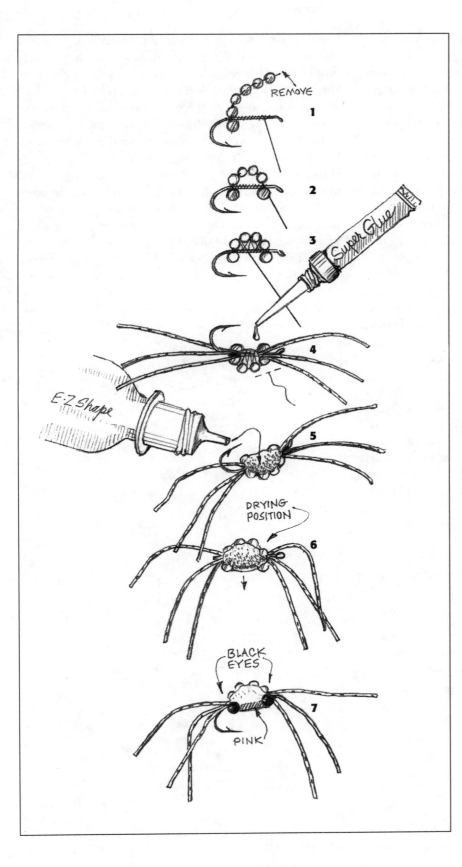

1. Attach the thread to a #6 hook. Be sure to cover the entire hook shank with a base of thread, then tie one end of the bead chain (six beads) onto the rear portion of the hook shank. (The other end of chain should be facing away from you after this step has been completed.)

2. Bend the bead chain around to the front of the hook, and secure it just behind the eye of the hook.

3. Wrap the thread back and forth several times around the hook and the bead chain, crisscrossing the opening, to construct support for the body.

4. Rotate the hook in the vise, then prepare the legs. Cut three legs to length (about half the length of a Sili-leg works well). Place the three pieces of Sili-legs across the body of the fly, and make a couple of wraps. Before completing any additional wraps, spread the legs, separating them to improve the appearance of the crab. Finish securing the legs, and tie off the thread. Add a drop or two of superglue to the hook shank and the body portion of the fly. This prevents the body from twisting on the hook.

5. Coat the top of the body with E-Z Shape Sparkle Body (sand crab).

6. Rotate the fly in the vise, coat the bottom of the body with E-Z Shape Sparkle Body (white), and set the fly aside to dry overnight. Position the crab as shown while it is drying. This maintains its shape.

7. Paint the front edge of the body between the eyes with pink fingernail polish, and paint the eyes using black fingernail polish.

Soda Straw Shrimp

Through the years, I have tied and fished a variety of shrimp patterns. Some of these flies were exact replicas of established patterns; others were my own creations. I was never satisfied with the bodies on my shrimp, however. The antennae, eyes, and legs were never a problem, but the body just didn't look realistic enough to suit me.

While at the International Fly Tier's Symposium in New Jersey, I had the opportunity to swap tips, tricks, and ideas with tiers from around the world. During the two-day affair, I was fortunate to spend a little time with an innovative tier and superb fly caster from the Netherlands named Sepp Fuchs. Sepp was tying a great-looking shrimp pattern. He cut a section from a plastic soda straw, then attached it over the top of the dubbed body. The antennae, eyes, legs, and dubbed body of his shrimp pattern were produced from conventional materials, but the body was unique. I liked the idea of using a plastic soda straw, and as is generally the case with creative tiers, finding a new material sent me racing back to the vise.

When tying my Piping Squid (described later), I slide the piping over the underbody, rather than tying a section of the piping over it. When I began experimenting with this new material, I did the same thing. After tying on the eyes, antennae, legs, and underbody, I stretched the rib portion of the straw by pulling on the ends, cut a section of the ribbed area to match the length of the hook, and trimmed both ends of the piece to a sharp point. After trimming the piece a couple more times with scissors, the plastic body fit perfectly between the eyes and over the underbody. I reattached the thread, tied down the end of the plastic body just behind the eye of the hook, and tied off the thread.

I later realized that the body required a little more effort to prevent it from being torn loose when the shrimp was fished. I now apply a little Goop over the top of the underbody before slipping the plastic body over it. I also make a few wraps around the end of the body, then pull the tip of the plastic back over these wraps and make additional wraps to better secure the front of the soda straw body before tying off the thread.

Materials List

HOOK:	Mustad 34011, #1/0, #2/0, or #3/0.
THREAD:	Red or orange 3/0 waxed.
UNDERBODY:	Pink chenille.
OUTER BODY:	Section of a bendable soda straw, trimmed to shape and colored with fingernail polish.
EYES:	Made from heavy monofilament, five-minute epoxy, and black fingernail polish (see drawing).
LEGS:	Dark brown deer tail over light green Krystal Flash tied onto the hook shank between the eyes.
ANTENNAE:	Two long, narrow grizzly hackles tied along either side under the eyes.
HACKLE:	Large webbed grizzly hackle.
GOOP:	Applied to the top of the underbody.

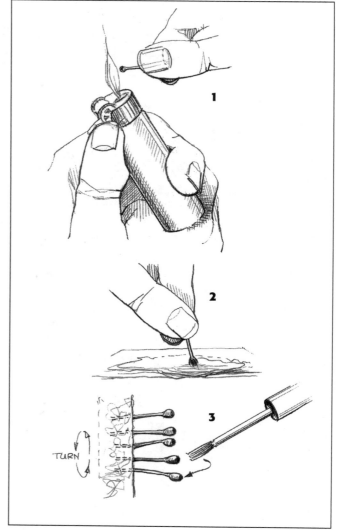

FIRST DRAWING

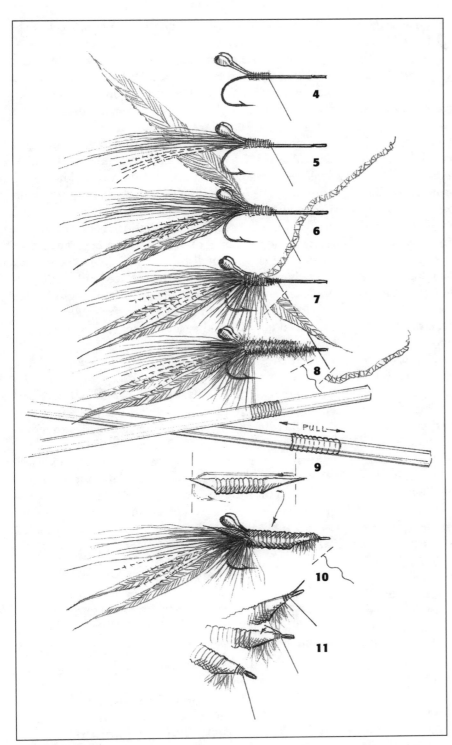

SECOND DRAWING

FIRST DRAWING

1. Cut 60- to 80-pound monofilament into pieces about $1^1/_4$ inches long, then melt one end of each piece with a lighter.

2. Dip the melted end of the mono-filament piece into five-minute epoxy. I use faster-setting epoxy because it turns amber over time, and I think amber-colored eyes are more realistic than clear eyes.

3. Stick the other end of the monofila-ment into the side of the Styrofoam disc on a drying wheel, and turn the eyes until they harden. Coat the Soda Straw Shrimp eyes twice with epoxy, let harden, and paint the end of each eye with black.

SECOND DRAWING

4. Attach the thread at the rear of the hook, and tie in the eyes.

5. Tie six to eight strands of light green Krystal Flash onto the top of the hook just behind the eyes, followed by twelve to fifteen strands of dark brown deer tail.

6. Tie a long, narrow grizzly hackle along either side of the head, then tie in the large webbed grizzly hackle that will form the legs.

7. Wrap several turns of the large hackle, then tie it off and remove the excess from the top of the fly. Attach the length of pink chenille.

8. Bring the thread forward, and wrap the chenille around the hook, form-ing the underbody. Tie off the che-nille, remove the excess, and tie off the thread.

9. Pull the ends of the straw to extend the rib, then trim the plastic piece to shape.

10. Apply a little Goop over the top of the underbody. Slip the section of soda straw over the underbody, re-attach the thread, secure the front of the body, and tie off the thread.

11. These three steps show you how to secure the front of the soda straw body before tying off.

Krystal Flash Fly

In his saltwater fly-tying video, Lefty Kreh makes a statement regarding the use of Krystal Flash. Lefty says, "You don't want to overwhelm your flies with flash. Most of the time, four or five strands are all that you need." I would be the last person to disagree with the old master, but his statement triggered an idea. What would happen if I designed a fly that was tied almost entirely with Krystal Flash?

The technique used for the body had been established for some time. I had combined Krystal Flash and epoxy to make up bodies on shad flies, soft-hackle flies fished in my local trout stream, and several other saltwater patterns. This type of body is very durable and adds a little flash to the fly. After locating a couple of stainless steel hooks, I wound fifteen to eighteen full-length strands of Krystal Flash around the hook shanks, tied off the thread, coated them with thirty-minute epoxy, and put them on the drying wheel to harden.

After the epoxy hardened, I placed one of them in the vise and set my Krystal Flash stand within easy reach. Next, I cut off a good-size bunch of chartreuse Krystal Flash, folded it, and cut it in half. I worked the Krystal Flash back and forth in my fingers so that the ends would be of varied lengths, folded it again, cut it in half, and tied the material onto the front of the hook. I was about to tie off the thread when I decided that this pattern needed a little more flash. I tied in more chartreuse Krystal Flash under the hook to form the throat and tied off the thread. A pair of stick-on eyes and a little more epoxy completed the pattern.

The results of the first field test were mixed. The fly had wonderful action in the water, and the fish seemed to love it, but more often than not, the Krystal Flash wing got tangled around the point of the hook. I made more flies, tying the wing farther back on the hook. They fouled less, but the wonderful action was gone, and so were the fish. After numerous attempts to work out the "bugs" in the design, I tried putting a little FisHair under the Krystal Flash wing, as well as on top of it. This solved the fouling problem without killing the wonderful action.

As the season was winding down, I was invited to fish Long Island. By this time, I was testing several new designs, but I took the time to fish the Krystal Flash fly while fly-casting off the South Shore. As expected, it was inhaled by several striped bass, including a large fish that put me well into the backing twice.

Several months later, I spent a couple of weeks fishing the Bahama flats. As is always the case, I had several more new patterns that I was anxious to field-test. By the end of the first week, I had adequately tested the new creations. Now I could pick through the 400 to 500 hundred flies I had brought along and fish a few of my well-established favorites.

It didn't take very long before I was attaching a Krystal Flash fly onto the end of a fine wire leader. After covering 30 to 40 yards of the warm, knee-deep water, I spotted a fish. The barracuda wasn't more than 15 feet off the water's edge in about 6 inches of water. I dropped the fly a few feet in front of the toothy critter, let it sink for a couple of seconds, then began a fast retrieve. I never saw the fish make its move. One second it was lying perfectly still at the surface, and a split second later it was attached to the end of my line. The fish screamed the reel, zigzaging across the shallow flat. It wallowed and jumped several times before I was able to land it.

After carefully releasing the fish, I took a good look at the Krystal Flash fly. As usual, the wing required a little attention, but the fly was still fishable. It had held up much better than expected. In fact, it took two more fish before the fourth one finally destroyed it.

I've caught dozens of different species of saltwater game fish on Krystal Flash streamers tied in a variety of colors. I've taken a few good fish on white, blue and white, and pink, but my favorites are all predominantly green. The green Krystal Flash streamers have saved the day more than once, taking fish when conventional patterns failed.

Materials List

HOOK:	#2 to #3/0, 2XL saltwater hook.
THREAD:	White 3/0 flat waxed nylon.
BODY:	Pearl Krystal Flash, coated with thirty-minute epoxy.
WING:	Small amount of chartreuse FisHair under a generous amount of chartreuse Krystal Flash. A little medium green FisHair is tied over the top of the first two layers to complete the wing.
THROAT:	Chartreuse Krystal Flash.
EYES:	Your choice.

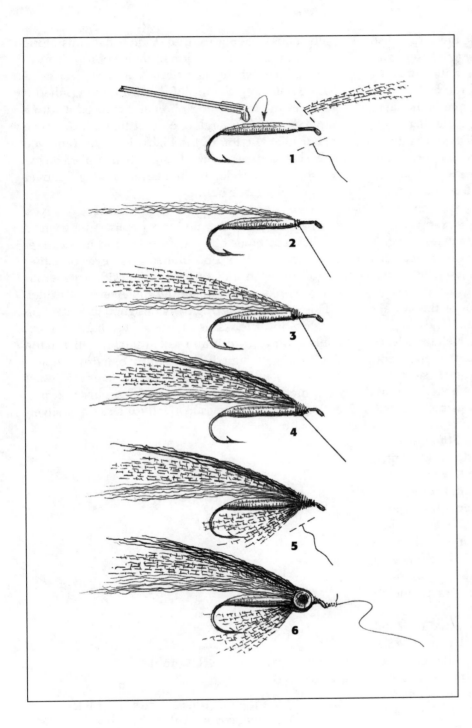

1. Attach the thread, and tie on fifteen to eighteen strands of pearl Krystal Flash. Cover the hook shank with pearl Krystal Flash, remove the excess, and tie off the thread. Coat the body with thirty-minute epoxy, and put the fly on the drying wheel to harden.

2. After the body has hardened, reattach the thread, and tie on the chartreuse FisHair.

3. Tie a generous amount of chartreuse Krystal Flash over the top of the FisHair. The wing should be about twice the length of the hook.

4. Tie a small amount of medium green FisHair over the top of the wing.

5. Tie a little chartreuse Krystal Flash under the hook shank, and tie off the head.

6. Stick on a couple of eyes, and coat the head with thirty-minute epoxy.

Silversides Streamer

While the others were casting to the larger fish cruising the bay, Bobby Lindquist and I were pursuing much smaller quarry. We dragged the net along the bottom toward the right side of the launch site, lifted it, and carried our catch to the edge of the sand. The net yielded a variety of critters, including a few bunkers, dozens of sand eels, a jellyfish, and a good-size, very angry bluepoint crab, but the majority of our catch comprised hundreds of silversides.

Several weeks after returning home from the salt, I finally found time to review the slides and the frozen samples we had collected. After carefully examining the silversides, I determined that this particular baitfish is well named. However, the bright silver area that runs along the entire length of its body isn't just a line; it has a particular shape. Only the head, the eye, the rib cage, and a thin line extending to the base of the tail are bright silver. The rest of the baitfish is rather drab.

I started looking for a material to match the silvery sides of these baitfish. After a period of trial and error, I found some Mylar ribbon at a local craft store and purchased a roll. The glimmer ribbon looked promising, but when I attempted to trim it to shape, it frayed, making it impossible to handle. The fraying problem was solved by applying a thin coat of Softex to both sides of the ribbon. After some additional trimming, the piece of ribbon was finally secured to a hook, but I was still concerned that the ribbon would come apart when the streamer was fished. I applied a little epoxy to the hook shank and between the ribbon and then coated the body portion of the streamer with more epoxy. After the prototype hardened, I removed it from the wheel and examined it. The Mylar body looked great. Working out the remaining details of the design would be easy.

First, I tied a generous amount of white deer tail under the body. This changed the overall proportion of the streamer, so I rejected it. Next, I tied a little deer hair along the sides of the body. This retained the slender shape of the streamer, but it covered too much of the silver, so I reduced the amount of hair. This worked very well.

Silversides have a thin, dark line that runs along the top of the silvery portion of their bodies. To form this line, I used six to eight strands of black deer tail. I tied the hair onto the top of the head, then pulled it back over the top of the ribbon and secured it with a couple drops of superglue. Next, I tied a little green FisHair over the top of the black deer tail, removed the excess, and tied off the head. I then applied a couple drops of superglue to the FisHair to secure it over the top of the black hair.

The last dominant feature of silversides is the eyes, which are bright silver with black pupils. After trying a few different types of eyes, I decided to use a silver Prizma stick-on eye. I positioned these eyes on either side of the head and secured them with a generous coat of epoxy to complete the Silversides Streamer.

This streamer was originally designed to imitate silversides, but it looks like many of the baitfish commonly found in fresh and salt water. It will catch a wide variety of game fish, including bluefish, stripers, large trout, and smallmouth bass, to name a few. I recommend that you tie up a good supply and present them to any species that will eat a slender, silver-sided baitfish.

Materials List

HOOK:	#1 or #2, 2XL saltwater hook.
THREAD:	White 3/0 flat waxed nylon.
BODY:	Made from 1-inch-wide silver Mylar ribbon, coated with Softex.
BELLY:	White deer tail, tied very sparse.
WING:	Green FisHair over six to eight strands of black deer tail.
EYES:	Silver Prizma stick-on eyes.

SUPERGLUE, FIVE-MINUTE EPOXY, AND THIRTY-MINUTE EPOXY:
Used on the head and body.

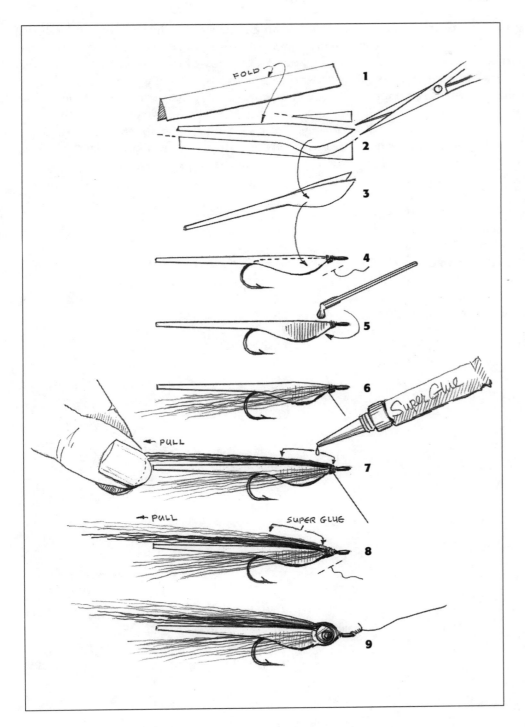

1. To keep the Mylar ribbon from fraying, apply a thin coat of Softex before cutting it to the desired shape. After the Softex has dried, cut a 2³/₄-inch length of ribbon, and fold it in half.

2. Cutting on the side away from the fold, cut the belly portion of the ribbon to the desired shape, then taper the top to a point.

3. The ribbon is ready to be tied onto the hook.

4. Attach the thread, prewrap the hook shank with thread, tie the ribbon onto the hook, and tie off the thread.

5. Coat the body portion of the ribbon with five-minute epoxy. A little epoxy is also applied along the hook shank, inside the ribbon. Put the fly on the drying wheel to turn until it has hardened. Apply epoxy *only* to the heavy portion of the ribbon. Gluing the tail will make it stiff, destroying the action.

6. Tie a little white deer tail along both sides of the streamer. Keep the hair *sparse* so that it doesn't cover up the flashy appearance of the heavy portion of the ribbon.

7. Tie eight to ten strands of black deer tail onto the top of the head. Pull the hair tight over the top of the ribbon, and glue it into position using a few drops of superglue. Don't apply any glue beyond the rear of the hook.

8. Tie green FisHair onto the head and tie off the thread. Then pull it tight and apply glue, as in the previous step.

9. Attach a pair of stick-on eyes. Then coat the head with thirty-minute epoxy.

Piping Squid

I was having a difficult time getting my fly in front of a school of frenzied bluefish. The wind was blowing directly in my face, and the surf was pounding at my feet. Even when I was able to sneak in a long cast between gusts, I had little control over what my popper did on the water.

I decided it was time to try a new fly. I needed something that would cut the wind and sink the instant it touched down. After testing several other flies, I snapped a Piping Squid onto the end of the wire tippet and launched my line. The fly hit the water and sank, allowing me to work the fly in front of the fish before the surf trashed my presentation. It made all the difference. This time, a large bluefish got a good look at my offering, liked what it saw, and snatched my squid. During the next hour, I caught and released three more blues on the same fly—not the same pattern, the same fly. The school moved on, and my thoughts turned to hot coffee and breakfast. As I walked up the beach, I detached the Piping Squid and took a good look at it. The fly was chewed up a bit, but it was still fishable.

It's rare for a fly to survive the teeth of four bluefish. Many squid patterns have soft bodies that won't take much abuse. The body of the Piping Squid is coated with epoxy and stands up to the toothy critters. The epoxy also protects the plastic eyes. The arctic fox or lamb's wool collar soaks up water, so the fly sinks quickly. It also gives the fly an appetizing "breathing" action when you strip it. This action mimics the movement of a squid fluttering its caudal fins.

Materials List

HOOK:	Mustad 34011 or equivalent, #2/0 to #4/0.
THREAD:	White 3/0 flat waxed.
BODY AND HEAD:	Mylar piping.
TAIL:	White bucktail, over which is tied silver tinsel or Krystal Flash and natural red fox tail.
COLLAR:	Arctic fox tail or lamb's wool.
UNDERBODY:	Filler from Mylar piping.
NOSE:	Red thread.
EYES:	Plastic doll eyes.
WATERPROOF MARKERS:	Used to color the collar and body.
THIRTY-MINUTE EPOXY:	Used to coat the body and eyes.

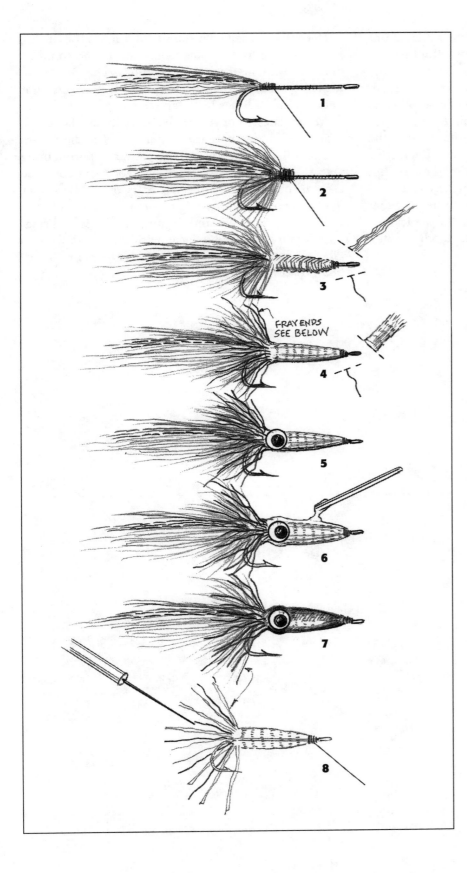

FRAY ENDS
SEE BELOW

1. Attach the thread, and tie on the tail. Begin with white deer tail, followed by six or eight strands of silver holographic tinsel. A small amount of red fox tail (comb out most of the underfur) is then tied over the top of the tinsel to complete the tail.

2. Tie on a collar of arctic fox tail around the base of the tail. Then apply a few drops of cement.

3. Using strands of the filler pulled from Mylar piping, wrap an underbody around the entire hook shank, and tie off the thread.

4. Apply a couple drops of Flexament to the head and underbody, and slide the piping over it. Attach the red thread to the head of the fly, tie down the end of the piping, and finish off the head.

5. Attach the plastic doll eyes using a hot glue gun. The hot glue can also be used to fill in the gap between the eyes.

6. Coat the entire body and eyes with a thin coat of epoxy. Put the lure on the drying wheel to turn until it hardens.

7. Apply the color using markers.

8. The piping is frayed *before* it is slid over the underbody.

Tuff Tail Streamer

I have seldom regretted having one of my creations torn to pieces by a predator with a mouthful of needle-sharp teeth. Having a fly ripped to pieces is always better than getting no hits at all. However, when another fish is within casting range and the fly attached to the end of the leader isn't fishable, I mind.

Durable flies are easy to tie. You simply coat the more fragile materials with several layers of epoxy or avoid using materials that are easily torn apart. But doing so often results in a fly that is lifeless as it is retrieved through the water. The trick is to tie a fly that will move but hold up when it is inhaled by a pickerel, pike, barracuda, bluefish, or a similar toothy critter.

Recently I received a sample of a new type of Bug Skin. Bug Skin is thin, pliable leather, treated so that it doesn't shrink after repeated wettings. This fine product has been around for a while, but the new version is quite different. It has been laminated with a thin layer of Mylar. These thin yet tough sheets are available in a variety of flashy patterns that look as if they were peeled off the sides of baitfish. After experimenting with the new Bug Skin, I determined that it could be used to concoct a very effective, very durable streamer fly—a new pattern deserving of the name Tuff Tail.

Bug Skin can be found in some fly shops and catalogs. If you have trouble locating this material, write to Chuck's Special Skins, Seven Springs Mountain Resort, 685 Broadway, Rockwood, PA 15557.

Materials List

HOOK:	Mustad 3407, #2/0, #3/0, or #4/0.
THREAD:	White 3/0 flat waxed nylon.
TAIL:	Metallic-finish Bug Skin coated with contact cement.
WING:	Black deer hair.
THROAT:	White artic fox fur with a little red wool tied directly under it.
EYES:	Round or oval doll eyes.
WATERPROOF MARKERS:	Used to color the Bug Skin.
SUPERGLUE:	Used to secure the tail to the hook.
FIVE-MINUTE EPOXY:	Used to coat the head and eyes.
FINGERNAIL POLISH:	Black on the top, red on the bottom of the head.

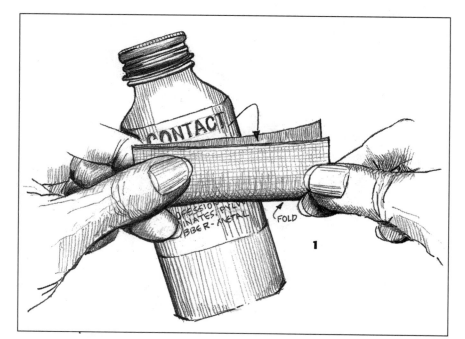

FIRST DRAWING

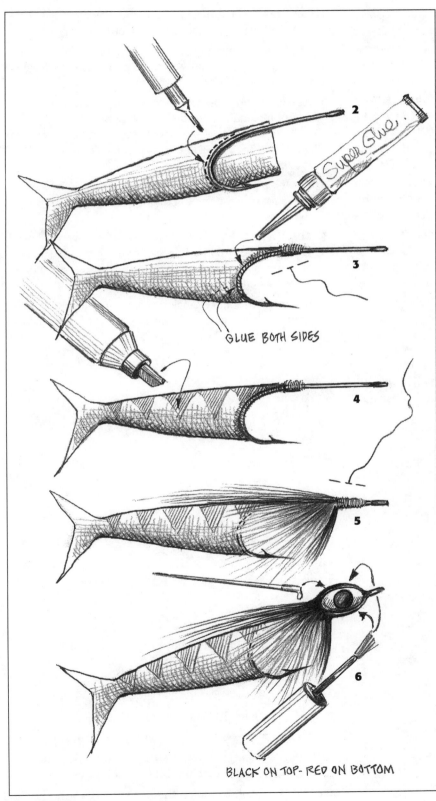

GLUE BOTH SIDES

BLACK ON TOP - RED ON BOTTOM

FIRST DRAWING

1. Apply a thin coat of contact cement to the back side of the Bug Skin. After the cement has set for a few minutes, fold the material and press it together.

SECOND DRAWING

2. The tails can be cut long and slim or short and fat. Proportion the tails to match the body shape of the baitfish you're attempting to imitate. After cutting the material to shape, trim the front of the piece to match the exact shape of the bend of the hook. The easiest way to do this is to lay the hook on top of the material and trace along the bend with a fine marking pen, then make the final cut.

3. Begin the tying process by wrapping thread around the bend and rear portion of the hook shank. Next, hold the tail in position and make a few wraps, securing the "tip" end of the tail piece to the hook, and tie off the thread. Apply superglue along the edge of the Bug Skin and the thread. After this first application, apply a second coat of superglue to both sides, and set it aside to dry.

4. After the superglue has dried, the Bug Skin can be colored with a permanent marker. Use your imagination when applying the color.

5. Finishing the streamer is simple. Reattach thread and tie a small bundle of black deer hair across the top of the fly. Next, tie a bunch of arctic fox fur under the shank of the hook, filling the open area inside the gap of the hook. Then tie in a little red wool to simulate the gills, and tie off the thread.

6. Attach a pair of doll eyes with a hot glue gun. Then coat the entire head with epoxy and let it harden. Applying a little black paint across the top of the head and a little red under it completes the Tuff Tail Streamer.

SECOND DRAWING

Fishy's Floater

When the surface is choppy, I've found that poppers and other flies that splash and make noise are generally the most productive. However, during those rare times when the sea is like a millpond, these flies seem to spook the fish rather than trigger strikes.

One of the most productive spinning lures I have cast on a calm sea is the Zara Spook. This surface plug doesn't make much of a commotion on the surface when it is retrieved, but its erratic side-to-side action often triggers explosive strikes from striped bass and bluefish. After fishing the Zara Spook for many years, I began to experiment with a variety of materials, hoping to come up with a fly with a similar action on the water. Fishy's Floater, a combination of tail, foam, and Mylar piping, fills that need.

The body of Fishy's Floater is shaped like the Zara Spook, and the fly has a similar action when retrieved by quickly stripping in the fly line a foot or two at a time. When the surface of the sea is glass smooth, I have done very well fishing this pattern. It rides high in the water and makes very little commotion when it is retrieved. If it is retrieved so that it imitates the erratic swimming action of a feeding baitfish, this fly-rod version of the Zara Spook produces explosive strikes when other flies are refused.

1. Cut a piece of foam as shown in the drawing. Then cut a slit halfway into it and glue the foam onto the kinked hook with superglue.

2. Trim the foam to shape and to accommodate the inside diameter of the piping.

3. Attach the thread and tie in the tail, using any combination of materials. Make the tail the same length as the body. Next, push the piping over the underbody, tie down the end of the piping at the base of the tail, and tie off the thread.

4. Pull the piping forward, and cut it to length. Reattach the thread, secure the front of the piping behind the eye of the hook, and tie off.

5. Attach a pair of black, half-bead plastic eyes with a hot glue gun. Then apply a thin coat of thirty-minute epoxy to the body and eyes, and turn it on a drying wheel until it has hardened.

6. Use markers and fingernail polish to complete the details. After the coloring is finished, apply a second thin coat of epoxy.

Materials List

HOOK:	Mustad 9082S, #2/0 kinked popper hook.
THREAD:	White 3/0 flat waxed nylon.
UNDERBODY:	Any closed-cell foam.
OVERBODY:	Large, pale blue Mylar piping. Other colors may be used to make up variations of this creation.
TAIL:	Your choice.
EYES:	Black half-bead plastic eyes.
THIRTY-MINUTE EPOXY:	Used to coat the body and eyes.
WATERPROOF MARKERS AND FINGERNAIL POLISH:	Used when detailing around the eyes and gills.
SUPERGLUE:	Used to attach the underbody to the hook.

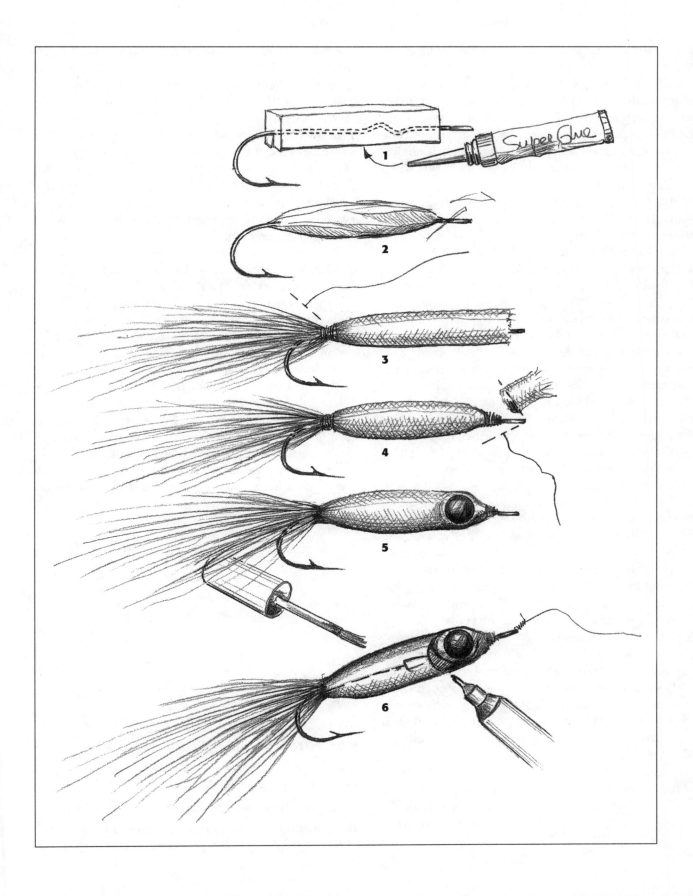

Shad Fly

A productive shad fly or two may be a contributing factor, but water conditions largely determine the success or failure of a shad fisher. A particularly cold spring can delay the run, because the fish won't arrive until the water temperature is to their liking. If the water temperature is fine and the fish are in, but the water is high and off-color, it may be difficult, if not impossible, to get a fly to the fish. I have had years when the fishing was wonderful, and years when I caught few, if any, fish during the spring shad run. If the water is fishable and the shad are in, then you can devise a strategy to catch them.

Choice of fly line is dictated by water conditions. If water levels are low, it is often possible to fish a floating line. However, if you are presenting a shad fly in more than a few feet of water, a sinking-tip line is required. A short length of lead-core line tied between the fly line and the leader will also do the job.

When fishing for the smaller hickory shad, a 5-weight outfit is adequate. My choice when pursuing the American shad is an 8-weight outfit. A slightly heavier rod, reel, and line may be fished, but I don't recommend going lighter. The heavier outfits shorten the battle, putting less stress on these fish. Since the majority of shad are released by choice or must be released by law, fishing lighter outfits is not a good idea.

When presenting a fly to shad, the first step is to throw away the rule book on proper presentation. Casting a shad fly upstream, then mending the line to achieve a drag-free presentation, will not catch shad. The best way to present a fly to this species is to position yourself upstream of an area that looks as if it might hold a few fish. Once in position, cast slightly down and across the current, let the current carry the fly downstream, and swing the fly across the area where the fish are holding.

Some strikes will come while the fly is swinging cross-current, but most fish take after the line has completely straightened out. After the line has straightened, just stand there with a good grip on the rod. Since you and the quarry are in a direct line in relation to each other, strikes feel as if someone is trying to yank the rod out of your hands.

If you get a strike and fail to hook the fish, retrieve a few feet of line, then slowly return the line to the water. It is likely that four to six fish were within striking distance of your fly. One of them took the offering but was not hooked. By taking the fly away from the fish and then slowly returning it to them, you are putting it back under their noses. Frequently, the fly is taken the instant it is within reach of the same fish that struck or another fish in its school.

In the thirty years that I have fished for hickory and American shad, I have learned that two flies are much more productive than one. Obviously, two shad flies do not cast as well as one, particularly when fishing a 5-weight outfit. It also takes a little more time to rig the two flies. However, far more shad will be taken when fishing the tandem rig.

If you are fortunate enough to have these silvery fish in nearby rivers or streams, I strongly suggest that you tie up a couple dozen of these simple flies, rig two of them onto the end of a leader, and present them to the shad. Shad are strong for their size. They put a bend in the long rod, always putting up a good battle, and occasionally they even jump.

All these flies are tied with the same white tail, but the bodies and heads can be tied in a variety of colors. When fishing for American shad, I have had the best results with pearl and red, but I have also taken fish on light green and red. Hickory shad take pearl- or light green–bodied flies with red heads, but this species seems to prefer a pearl body with a pink head. Experiment with different colors. It's fun, and doing so makes your fly box more colorful.

Materials List

HOOK:	#8 or #10 wet-fly hook.
THREAD:	Bright red 3/0 flat waxed.
BODY:	Pearl or light green Krystal Flash.
TAIL:	White rabbit or arctic fox.
EYES:	Silver bead chain.
HEAD:	Red fingernail polish.
THIRTY-MINUTE EPOXY:	Applied to the body and head.

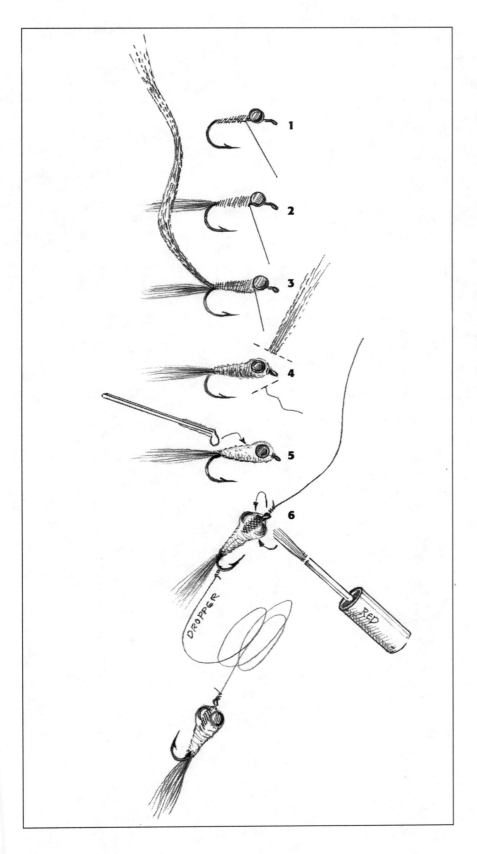

1. Attach the thread, and tie on a pair of bead-chain eyes to the front of the hook.

2. Tie in the tail, using white arctic fox or rabbit fur.

3. Tie in eight to ten strands of pearl Krystal Flash.

4. Wrap the Krystal Flash around the hook shank, forming a tapered body. Also wrap the Krystal Flash between the eyes, X-ing the material so that the gap between the eyes is covered. Pull the end of the Krystal Flash forward, tie it off, remove the excess, and tie off the head.

5. Coat the body and head of the fly with epoxy, and turn it on the drying wheel until it hardens.

6. A little red fingernail polish on the top and bottom of the head completes this pattern. Also shown is how the dropper and the second fly are attached to the first.

Fly-Tying Materials: Tips and Suggestions

Aero-Gloss. Used to coat the wing material in some patterns. This product is found in hobby shops (it's usually used when building model airplanes) and is best applied using a disposable foam brush. Two or three coats are required.

balsa wood. These 3-foot-long sticks of soft wood are available at most craft and hobby stores. I've tied hundreds of poppers, fancy dragonflies, and even extended-body mayfly imitations using balsa wood sticks.

Bug Skin. The only material that seems to work when tying Tuff Tails is Bug Skin. If you can't find it in fly-tying catalogs or at fly shops, write to Chuck's Special Skins, Seven Springs Mountain Resort, 685 Broadway, Rockford, PA 15557.

E-Z Shape Sparkle Body. The E-Z Shape products are superior, but if you can't find them, use acrylic fabric paints found in craft stores.

eyes. Check out the selection in craft stores. Doll eyes come in a wide variety of styles, colors, and sizes. Purchase them in bulk and save money. The half-bead plastic eyes are usually displayed with the doll eyes.

Faux Fur. This craft store item can be substituted for other dubbing material.

fingernail polish. The blacks, greens, and browns used by tiers aren't usually found in the displays of "designer" nail polish. Buy the cheap stuff at chain stores.

Flexi-floss, Super Floss, Spanflex. All these materials can be substituted for one another. Some can be split to make thinner strands. All are available in catalogs.

hopper foam. I prefer kickboard foam, but most high-density foams can be used. Kneeling pads, available at garden shops, are a little more expensive but make great flies. I've also used some packing foams. Check out toy stores for items made from high-density foam.

interfacing. Interfacing makes great wing material when coated with Aero-Gloss, but other thin, porous fabrics or ribbons can also be used. Even an old pair of pantyhose can be turned into super wing material.

Lipped Popper lips. Acrylic plastic sheets (available at craft stores), sections cut from discarded hook boxes, and any thin, clear plastic that is easy to cut can be used. Look at the plastic items you throw away; many of them are usable.

plastic canvas. Plastic canvas is available at craft stores. It comes in a variety of colors, which makes no difference, since the underbodies made from this product are covered with dubbing. More importantly, it comes in several different sizes.

plastic worm hooks. This hook is sold in most sporting goods stores (not fly shops). It is a popular hook used by bass fishers when rigging plastic worms, lizards, and crayfish.

sand. Although I suggested that sand from the bottom of your local trout stream be used for the Stone Caddis, any type of sand will do. It may actually be illegal to collect materials from the trout waters in your state.

sandpaper pointer. A sheet of sandpaper and a small block of wood can be used, but I prefer the pointer, used by artists to sharpen their pencils. Sandpaper pointers can be purchased at any art supply store. Large emery boards also work well when sanding and shaping balsa wood bodies.

sheet foam. The thinner sheet foams are a common craft store item, but the thicker sheets may be difficult to find. Try cutting hopper foam or the soles of flip-flops into the desired thickness.

Sili-legs. This is the same material used for "skirts" on spinner baits and jigs fished by bass anglers. Replacement skirts are often available at sporting goods stores, even ones that don't specialize in fly-fishing gear. This popular material is easy to find in a variety of colors and sizes. Check out the fly-tying catalogs.

silver Mylar ribbon. I prefer a ribbon made by Prasent called "glimmer" silver, but it is difficult to find. Any metallic Mylar ribbon can be used. Most of the time I use the silver, but other colors can be used to tie variations of the Silversides Streamer.

soda straws. Remember that you need the bendable straws. This item comes in several sizes and a variety of colors, making it possible to tie some interesting shrimp patterns.

waterproof markers. Any brand of waterproof marker can be used. Purchase the cheapest ones, since you're not going to be drawing with them, just adding some color to a few flies.

Z-Lon. The core removed from larger Mylar piping (not the soft cotton fiber) is a great substitute for Z-Lon. I often use it for wings on everything from large dragonflies to tiny mayfly spinners.